GOLDEN VISA

I0409187

Mindset & Strategies on Entrepreneurship, Global Citizenship, and Nomadic Lifestyle

Melchor Tatlonghari

ISBN: 9798862332186
First Edition: 2023

Dedication

To my wife, my confidant, best friend, travel companion, business partner, constant inspiration, and love of my life.

Additional Resources

YouTube Channel: https://www.youtube.com/@aeyandmel
Links: https://linktr.ee/mel3kings
Website: https://www.melchortatlonghari.com/
Medium: https://medium.com/@meltatlonghari3

We document our travels and our global nomadic lifestyle on our YouTube channel. Come say 'hi' and connect with us.

Preface

I have always dreamed about the nomadic lifestyle, quitting my job and leaving it all behind to travel the world. It was always something to do "down the road." When I first started my career more than a decade ago, this was one of the end goals that I aspired to. I wanted to explore the world's natural beauty, visit different wonders of the world, meet diverse people of different cultures, eat all types of cuisine, and drink Piña colada by the beach without any worries. Hakuna Matata.

A decade had passed and it was still a dream of mine, but it felt like I wasn't any closer to making that dream a reality. There was always something that came up and disrupted the plan—bills that needed to be paid or unexpected family events that took priority. I realised that every time I put the dream on a pedestal and said "one day," it reaffirmed my inner subconscious belief that it would always be out of reach. Wanting and dreaming about becoming a nomad created a divide between myself and taking action. As long as I didn't commit to taking any action, something will always comes up.

I had become a corporate drone, mindlessly climbing through the ranks and earning a paycheque month after month. Although my work had an impact, it had become dull and soul-crushing. As a Software Engineer by trade, sitting in front of a screen for 8-10 hours a day felt more exhausting more than ever on top of being locked down for two years during the Coronavirus pandemic. Truth be told this wasn't what I envisioned as a "well-lived life." Yes, it paid the bills and there was food on the table, but something was missing. I began questioning, "Isn't there more to life than this?"

To fill this void, I quickly fell into materialism and pursued hedonic pleasures. I would buy things I didn't really need in order to get a quick adrenaline rush, only to be left feeling bored and dissatisfied again shortly after.

Soon enough, my dissatisfaction escalated into seeking adrenaline rushes through more expensive activities, such as overseas holiday trips. Initially, these trips lasted 2-3 days, but as my uneasiness grew, so did the duration of my getaways—stretching to a week at a time. It was becoming more and more unsustainable each time. But the thought of returning to the proverbial cubicle and working the traditional 9-5, Monday to Friday, became increasingly unnerving, I was looking for an escape as I couldn't imagine doing this for another 20-30 years. The worst part was, regardless of what I did or where I went, Mondays would always still arrive, I still had to get back in to the office, and I was still stuck in the monotonously boring 9-5 life. Was this really what life was meant to be? Trading our lives for 11 months of work each year, only to take a couple of weeks off before diving back in? I knew there had to be more.

I've always been a numbers guy. From the day I started working, I constantly tracked my finances down to every dollar. Deep down, I knew there was an end goal—it wasn't just about increasing the numbers in my bank account for no bigger purpose. One day, as I looked at the numbers, I realised that I could sustain this lifestyle long enough while pursuing a completely different path. It was just a matter of taking the plunge, but it was a scary and unnerving thought.

I had seen others follow the same blueprint. Some had stayed in corporate for almost three decades and were still stuck in the rat race—facing the same issues year after year. Bills kept piling up, inflation caught up with them, and hedonic pleasures remained their only escape from mundane everyday life. I knew I didn't want to be like them, and it was the current path I was threading.

It was only when I made the decision and committed that everything slowly fell into place. It wasn't just a dream or something I second-guessed —I made a clear decision with conviction in every fibre of my being. I told my wife, April, "We're ending our lease, packing our bags, and traveling around the world while we pursue our wildest dreams." To her credit, my wife had always been my other half and that day further solidified it. She had been thinking about the same things as me, she was growing restless with how we are currently living our lives but was worried about bringing it up. She argued that I had a promising career ahead of me—why risk it all now? I told her, "I can't imagine living like this for another 30-40 years, only to end up in a retirement home full of regrets." She understood because, deep down, she had always felt the same way.

Once we were on the same boat, we took swift action. I resigned from my job, informed my landlord about breaking the lease, and started packing our belongings while storing some of them. A good friend offered to watch our lovely dog back at home—a stroke of blessing as we had been constantly worried about where we could leave our furry friend. It's funny how the universe aligns perfectly when you've made up your mind and decide it's time to take action and live life on your own terms.

This book is one of the products that came from that decision. We've built several businesses and brands while on the road. The book you hold in your hands is a collection of knowledge, mindset, and strategies that we have personally used, gathered, and experienced over the years— strategies that finally enabled us to make the leap and hopefully will empower you to do the same.

My hope is that you'll realise there's much more to life than the conventional blueprint society has provided us, which typically involves graduating, finding a job, getting married, buying a house, and finally retiring. I do not judge or fault following the traditional path, to each is his own, but to the mavericks and pioneers who think there is another way I say: "Let's begin this journey of self-discovery and how you can start living your best life."

How This Book is Structured

In this book, I aim to provide a comprehensive guide to the nomad entrepreneur mindset and lifestyle. I recognise that there are already numerous resources available on the internet regarding finding accommodations, meetups, and travel hacks. I do not aim to repeat what is easily readily accessible just to add more pages to my book. I aim to deliver as much value to you as I possibly can, without boring you with the details that you may have already encountered online. I will, instead, delve into subjects that are often overlooked but essential for adopting a nomadic lifestyle. The topics here have timeless relevance to this way of life.

- Part 1, we will discuss the necessary mindset shift required to embrace this lifestyle fully. If you assume that becoming a nomad is similar to just having a long vacation you might be in for a rude awakening or what they call 'gomad' . Without the right mindset, it can be challenging to make the necessary adjustments and find success as a nomad.

- Part 2, we will explore the financial aspects that need to be considered when transitioning into a nomadic lifestyle. This includes organising your finances, generating passive income, thinking in compounding terms, and ensuring everything is in order before embarking on this journey.

- Part 3, we will focus on core competencies that are crucial for any business venture you wish to pursue as a nomad. These competencies will empower you and provide a solid foundation for your entrepreneurial endeavours regardless of what business or brand you want to build for yourself.

- Part 4 will introduce essential travel hacks that can make your nomadic life more convenient and efficient. These tips and tricks will help you navigate different countries and cities with ease.

- Part 5, we will provide a sneak peek into what life after being a nomad might look like. This section will explore potential opportunities and challenges that may arise once you decide to settle down or transition into something new.

As someone who loves to read, I completely relate to the frustration of books that begin with great momentum but then fail to maintain it. It often feels like they could have been condensed into a much shorter article instead of dragging on unnecessarily to a book. To avoid falling into this trap, I have carefully structured this book into distinct parts. Each part is designed to provide maximum value without wasting your time on a single topic for too long.

But first, we begin with why you wouldn't want to be a nomad.

INTRODUCTION

Nomad or Go-mad

"Life is either a daring adventure or nothing at all." - Helen Keller

Reverse Bucket List

There's a saying that it's easier to know what you don't want to be compared to knowing what you want to be. With so many choices in life, it's difficult to make a definitive decision about what we want to be. However, it is often much easier to start eliminating certain paths and decision points based on what we don't like. Personally, I didn't know what

I wanted to be, but I was clear about the things I didn't want for my life. I didn't want to be stuck working for someone else forever, confined to one location for long periods of time. I didn't want to look back and regret not exploring all my options. Most importantly, I didn't want my twilight years filled with advice for younger people on how they should travel more; instead, I wanted a highlight reel of my own adventures and experiences around the world. I didn't want my body deteriorating while still being forced to work, trading my time for money.

My dad passed away at relatively young age, he was only 64 years old. He worked his entire life to provide for us and saved every penny he could until retirement. Sadly, only four years after retiring, he had a heart attack. While I admired his dedication and sacrifice for our family, I didn't want the same life for myself. Saving everything until the end only to have it cut short in an instant was not the path I wanted to take.

Although uncertain about what exactly I wanted to become, I knew exactly what I didn't want. And so began my journey as a nomadic entrepreneur—a global citizen not dependent on an employer for sustenance. My goal was to see the world and create something valuable for society. The book you are currently reading is one of the products that emerged from this journey—a constant balance between building and living at the same time. It wasn't a choice between one or the other; I wanted both. I want you to know that this is possible, and I will guide you through the mindset shifts, financial management, and necessary skills to live a boundless life.

Rose Tinted Glasses Can't See Red Flags

When I first embarked on my journey as a nomadic entrepreneur, I was initially shocked by how disconnected it was from my expectations versus reality. Like many things on social media, it had been heavily romanticised. Everyone seemed to only post about the positives and never revealed the challenges. It was all about beautiful beaches, delicious food, and exciting travels without any mention of the reality. While there is truth to the positive aspects, making life-changing decisions cannot be solely based on upsides. It's like buying a house solely based on the aesthetics without any consideration to its plumbing—it's important to see the complete picture when making life-changing decisions.

As I explored further on my personal journey, I realised what I didn't want and began discerning what I truly desired. My aim is to empower you to make informed choices without the rose-tinted glasses of social media distorting your perception of reality. In this chapter, I will debunk common misconceptions about living this lifestyle by sharing cautionary tales.

Serendipity Events

Nassim Nicholas Taleb's book *The Black Swan: The Impact of the Highly Improbable* discusses how predictability eliminates the chance for serendipitous events that can change possibly our lives for the better. By sticking rigidly to routines, avoiding uncertainty, and not taking calculated risks, we miss out on potential opportunities and personal growth. Being a nomad removes this predictability completely and exposes us to constant change in our daily lives.

Living as a nomad comes with both advantages and disadvantages. On one hand, we may stumble upon life-changing events such as meeting a potential partner or discovering a million-dollar business idea. On the other hand, we are also exposed to negative events like contracting life-threatening diseases or encountering dangerous situations in unfamiliar places.

Managing this constant change requires a strong mindset. The chaos of living in hostels one week, beachfront accommodations the next, and co-living spaces after that can be overwhelming for those accustomed to stability. Going from having a ten-year plan to not knowing what the next month or week will look like requires mental preparation. This is not something any one can just prepare for in a short period of time.

Before committing to a nomadic lifestyle, I decided to do some trial runs within our own country. This way, if things didn't go as planned, we would have the support of friends and family nearby. We started by allowing our leases to expire and then moved to different cities. I purposely sought out work opportunities that required me to relocate to completely different parts of the country. We even took the leap and migrated to different countries on two separate occasions.

Even after experiencing all these changes, it was still difficult for me to determine if I was truly ready to become a full-fledged nomad. While traveling for work and changing apartments provided some sense of predictability, there were still aspects that I couldn't fully prepare for. For example, when working remotely, I knew when my contract would expire, what the new location would look like, and who I needed to speak with regarding logistics. These were simple details that provided some level of comfort.

However, as a nomad, everything changes. Language barriers become a daily obstacle, familiar foods are no longer easily accessible, transportation systems vary greatly from place to place, and reliable internet connection can be hard to come by. These are just a few examples of how the things we take for granted in our everyday lives suddenly become uncertain.

In order to successfully navigate this new lifestyle, it requires adaptability and a willingness to embrace the unknown. It means being open-minded and quickly adjusting to new environments and cultures. It's not always easy or glamorous, but for those who are willing to embrace the challenges that come with being a nomad, it can be an incredibly rewarding experience.

Slow Motion

When we experience uncomfortable or novel situations, our brains become hyper-aware, causing time to seemingly slow down. For example, a one-minute plank can feel like an eternity. As a nomad, time also slows down significantly due to the constant change and new experiences. A month can feel like two or three months compared to the rapid passage of time in our comfort zones back home.

Perceiving time differently can have both positive and negative effects on our mental state. It can feel like a prison sentence if we constantly question why we gave up our comfortable lives for this nomadic lifestyle. However, it can also inspire us with the belief that we have ample time to figure things out and accomplish anything given enough effort.

On top of these adjustments, there's also the added pressure of visa expiration looming over us every few months. This creates a unique perception of time where a day can feel much longer than its standard 24 hours as we constantly juggle managing our own internal state and the logistics of moving to another country constantly. Some nomads use this perceived extra time wisely by living their best life and making the most out of each day. However, others see it as a prison sentence that drives them mad (hence the word: Gomad). Adjusting to different time zones and managing the perception of time are crucial in effectively managing the nomadic lifestyle and its sustainability.

Silent Pressure

Unless you've completely cut ties with everyone back home without saying goodbye, people from your social circle will constantly ask about your life as a nomad and seek advice on how they can do it too. Initially, these inquiries may seem normal and expected. Friends and family naturally worry about your well-being and are curious about your experiences. It's important to provide them with the necessary reassurances.

However, the constant question from family members can also lead to feelings of fatigued. They may assume that you have all the answers to questions such as "What's your one-year or five-year plan?", "How do you handle visa applications while constantly moving?", and "When are you coming back?" These are things that you are still figuring out as you navigate your journey. The worry they have exponentially grows as more time passes you stay as a nomad. They imagine all sort of worst-case scenarios such as encountering a Cartel or even contracting Malaria. It becomes almost part of the job itself just to assure their concerns consistently.

While they continue their traditional jobs within the confines of a normal 9-5 routine, your world becomes highly romanticised in their eyes —similar to what they read in books and watch in the movies. They look at you with a hint of envy, and see you as 'living the life'. The reality is far from rainbows and butterflies; in fact, it's much tougher than most people realise. It's never just lounging around the beach and sight-seeing 24/7, it's about living a completely alternative lifestyle unknown to you or anyone you know.

The constant questioning becomes implicit pressure. It can become troublesome to manage on top of all the things going on and is something you didn't think you would have to deal with on top of everything the lifestyle demands of you.

Ain't No Vacation

One common misconception is that being a nomad is like taking an extended vacation. That couldn't be farther from the truth. While it is true that you will experience completely different sights and sounds, explore different places, and meet new people from different cultures, assuming it will feel like a vacation will lead to disappointment.

Being a nomad requires a completely different mindset compared to going on a holiday. When you become a nomad there will be several perspective shifts that will occur naturally that is far from how it would be when you are in an ordinary vacation.

The perspective shifts can be summarised below as TEST.

(T)ime - (E)at - (S)leep - (T)hings

Time

You become much more attuned to how you spend your time while being a nomad with regards to both work and leisure.

When I lived in Sydney, I didn't prioritise going to the Opera House or the Harbour Bridge because they were just ordinary buildings that I saw on my way to work. When you stay in a country for 2-3 months at a time, rushing to visit every tourist spot before leaving becomes less important. Instead, exploring the city evolves into more natural and organic way as you go about your daily life allows you to stumble upon these spots without feeling like a typical tourist. This create more sense of calm and belonging to where you currently are, similar to how you would be at your home place.

You might think at the beginning that I won't be spending much time about working during in this journey, this however quickly becomes blurry based on how you define work. Soon enough, you come to the realisation that you need to figure out how to earn money while traveling in order to sustain this lifestyle for a longer period. The guilt of not working may haunt you after the initial excitement subsides and the hedonic adaption sets in. If you tend to be a bit obsessive-compulsive, it can be difficult to truly unwind and enjoy leisure time without feeling compelled to do something productive for your business or to try to generate income. As a nomadic entrepreneur, sustainability becomes a primary consideration — how can you sustain this lifestyle without returning to the dreaded traditional 9-5 job?

Eat

As a tourist, you often seek out specific specialties and make an effort to eat as much of them as possible. For example, when in Singapore, you might try to find the best restaurants serving Chilli Crab. However, as a nomad, local delicacies become part of your everyday life. They lose their special label and simply become ordinary meals that you have for breakfast or lunch. Singapore Chilli Crab becomes just Crab. In your every day normal life, how often do you really eat crab? This change in mindset also means that you don't aim to indulge yourself by eating whatever you want in the shortest time frame possible because you are leaving in a couple of days. It is much more important to establish healthy eating routines and adapt to local cuisines, rather than having an indulge-now-worry-about-it-later mindset.

Sleep

Although this may seem liberating at first, the idea of not having to worry about waking up at a set time can actually disrupt your Circadian Rhythm and have a negative impact on your overall health in the long run.

Your Circadian Rhythm is essentially your body's internal clock that regulates various physiological processes, such as sleep-wake cycles, hormone production, and metabolism. When you consistently wake up at different times each day, it throws off this delicate balance and can lead to a host of health problems.

During my time in Thailand, I struggled with waking up early due to the unbearable morning heat. To make up for it, I would delay eating until later in the day when it was cooler outside. However, this disrupted sleep pattern led me to stay awake until 3am without being productive during those late hours. This lack of structure wasted valuable time and left me feeling tired and unrefreshed the following day.

It's becomes crucial not to underestimate the importance of a consistent sleep schedule, especially when constantly changing time zones and weather patterns.

Things

The reality of the Two-Luggage Constraint complicates the desire to hold onto as many things as you can. You simply cannot bring all your favourite things and gadgets with you. As you become a global citizen and travel around the world, you'll realise that no matter how much you want to bring all your favourite clothes, there will be a hard limit of around two luggages. Even if you can afford to pay for more luggage, the diminishing returns of carrying around more than two luggages as you hop from city to city and country to country become much clearer.

The focus then shifts from buying things to sustaining the lifestyle. As travel expenses, including flights, accommodations, food, and other essentials, come into play, it becomes natural for material possessions to slide down the priority list.

It's important to prioritise what truly matters when living a nomadic lifestyle. While it may be tempting to bring an extensive wardrobe and other things, it becomes more crucial to consider the practicality and limitations of traveling with only two luggages. By focusing on essentials and investing wisely, you can make the most out of your global adventures without compromising your financial stability.

Homesickness

It goes without saying that homesickness is a common experience for nomads, so I won't delve into it extensively here. However, what I will mention is that homesickness can extend beyond missing familiar people and places.

You may find yourself longing for simple things like your favourite spot on the couch or specific items that have become part of your daily routine, like your favourite pillow by the side of the bed. Constant change can make us yearn for even the most basic comforts we once took for granted back home. This aspect of homesickness was something I didn't anticipate when I first started my journey as a nomad entrepreneur, and might not be common knowledge for everyone planning to embark on the journey.

Chapter Summary: Nomad or Go-Mad?

- It's easier to start eliminating certain paths and decision points based on what we don't like rather than knowing exactly what we want to be
- Being a nomad is not like taking an extended vacation, it requires a different mindset and perspective shifts
- Living as a nomad exposes you to both positive and negative serendipity events and requires adaptability and embracing the unknown
- Time perception changes as a nomad, with days and months feeling longer than they do back home
- There is silent pressure from loved ones to have all the answers about your nomadic lifestyle
- Time, Eating, Sleeping, and Things (TEST) are all different as a nomad compared to being a tourist
- Homesickness goes beyond missing familiar faces and places, but also longing for basic comforts

It's You Against You

"Success is not final, failure is not fatal: It is the courage to continue that counts." - Winston Churchill

Writing a book for everyone on any demographic is simply not practical, a sound advice for a young 20 year old does not apply for someone on their retirement age, this applies for financial advice or any other advices really. When you tell someone you need to invest and wait for your money to compound to someone in a retirement home, it simply sounds satirical.

In the same vein, when you tell someone just starting their career how about the harshness of office politics and the fatigue that comes with working 9-5 over a span of decades, it falls on deaf ears. They are just starting their careers or just fresh out of college trying to find their footing in the world, they don't need a cynical or radical view of reinventing their life, they want to learn the hard way first and experience it first hand. So, before you continue reading I want to lay some ground works on my assumptions of who you are, your current state of life, and who this book might be intended for.

However, most of what I mention are not set in stone and is not a hard prerequisite for you to learn from this book, to not acknowledge outliers would be akin to shooting myself in the foot. These are just some guardrails so I have a some sort of semblance of who I think I'm writing for.

I also wanted to highlight that although this book is meant for a global audience, I based my metaphors and financial averages on the standards from a western point of view. As an Australian myself, I understand the desire to use familiar metaphors when discussing different currencies in various countries, however it does not make sense to write different metaphors for various currencies just to illustrate a point, when this book gets revised in different languages it will have accurate representation based on your geography, but for now let's talk in US dollars.

You've seen or have an idea of how corporate works

I assume you have been working for at least one to three years in a corporate setting, and the more experience you have, the better. My first job lasted three years, and during that time, I believed that my next company would be better. I didn't know it by then, but the following decade was bound to be filled with similar settings and politics, albeit with a fresh cast and stage.

Throughout my career, there has always been a common theme: office politics and facades. No matter where I go, there is always a rude client or boss to deal with. There is always that one co-worker who slacks off but takes credit for the team's hard work. And then there's that person who everyone knows is utterly incompetent but nobody has the courage to confront. The office environment may change, the people may be different, and even the type of work may vary, but beneath it all, the politics remain constant. It will always be a frustrating reality that many of us face in our professional lives.

To further emphasise this point, let me share a couple example from my own experience. In one company I worked for, there was a manager who constantly belittled his subordinates and took credit for their achievements. He would only show up in meetings when the team has actually finished the job, only to share in the spotlight. Despite numerous complaints about his behaviour, nothing was done because he had a close relationship with higher-ups in the company and to this day still gets away with this kind of behaviour. This unfairness and lack of accountability is unfortunately too common in corporate settings.

In another job, I encountered an office where everyone seemed to play by their own rules. There were no clear guidelines or expectations set by management, a "flat organisation" they called it, which led to confusion and inefficiency. Whoever was the loudest, and often the least capable, always took charge. It was frustrating to see so many talented individuals waste so much potential.

As I reflect on my own countless experiences, I've come to realise that there must be a better way. A way to escape the endless cycle of job hopping and dealing with toxic work environments.

I write for individuals who have experienced the corporate world at least once, if not multiple times, and have come to understand that it is not the only path to success. Consider this: you could dedicate 32 years, which is the average career length, only to be abruptly let go at the end of it. By that point, you may be older and unable to fully enjoy the rewards of your hard work. There is no rainbow at the end of the rain, at worst, inflation has caught up to your finances and you are left jobless at the ripe of retirement. If you still hold onto the belief that you will be traveling the world in your 60s or 70s with the same energy and outlook after retirement, I have some bad news for you my friend.

You have some sort of control

I assume you are not drowning in problems or baggage that you have no control over. I am no miracle worker, and I cannot magically make the life decisions made 10-20 years ago that are still haunting you go away. Travel is never a cure for anything; if you have issues at home, traveling does not change that fact.

In order to make a change in your life, you need to be in a position where you can make adjustments. It will always be hard to pour into a bucket filled with holes. If you read this book but have no capacity to implement anything, then you are just wasting time and effort. I strongly advise against this. If you have time to waste, it would be best to sort out your current predicament first, get your house in order first as they say. Otherwise, you may find that this book reads more like fiction than non-fiction.

You are not close-minded

I assume you are not close-minded and genuinely trying to find change and willing to make changes. Some of the ideas here might sound radical to you, it was the same for me at the beginning, if all the ideas are the same and does not introduce you a new perspective then what's the point? I do not aim to regurgitate the same mindset every one else has been sharing.

My blueprint was to become an overachieving employee, working tirelessly to earn as much money as possible and save whenever I could. I believed that this approach would sustain me in retirement. I pushed myself to the limit at work, climbing the corporate ladder with determination.

However, the mental strain and stress of my high-pressure lifestyle began to take its toll on me. My health rapidly deteriorated, and it became clear that something needed to change. When I finally took a moment to pause and reflect on my progress, I realised that despite my hard work, I still hadn't achieved the dream life I desired. Even though there were months I was working close to 16 hours a day, living a life at my own terms seemed farther than when I first started more than a decade ago. The corporate game is trading time for money and it's a losing game, you can only work so much in the hours of the day before something gives out. When something does give out—be it your health, your family, or your sanity—it's too late.

I received praise from companies who saw me as a rare talent - a unicorn - and they assured me that if I continued on this path for ten more years, success would be mine. But deep down, I knew that if I kept subjecting myself to the stress and toxicity of my environment for that long, it would likely result in further deterioration of my health rather than getting closer to achieving my goals.

As much as it pained me to admit it, my current approach wasn't leading me towards the life I truly desired. It was time for a different strategy, one that prioritised both my financial goals and my overall well-being.

What we underestimate is the toll stress takes on our bodies, when we are in constant fight or flight mode, our antibodies and immune system are just solely focused on keeping the engine running while we burn the candle at both ends. Stress takes a toll on our physical and mental well-being, often leaving us depleted and vulnerable. When we're constantly on edge, our bodies divert resources away from essential functions like repairing damaged cells or replenishing energy stores. Instead, they focus on immediate survival instincts, preparing us for fight or flight. Unfortunately, this means that vital processes necessary for long-term health and wellness are neglected. The body becomes a battleground between stress hormones and the immune system, resulting in increased susceptibility to illness and disease.

The danger lies in the fact that we often fail to recognise the signs of stress until they become too overwhelming to ignore. We push ourselves to the brink without realising that our bodies are crying out for relief.

Imagine a car running on empty with warning lights flashing all around. Ignoring these signals would ultimately lead to a breakdown or worse. Similarly, when we neglect self-care and ignore the warning signs of stress, our bodies eventually give in to exhaustion or illness.

I will not delve into the specifics of my illness, but I will say that it left me bedridden for nearly three months. This is the harsh reality of corporate life. As I lay in bed for days on end, contemplating what I did to get here, I realised that my managers and coworkers didn't give a damn. They didn't bother to visit. The bosses send you a get-well message and that's it, the company moves on. It was as if I had never existed; they had already found a replacement for me the minute I was gone. I thought to myself what if that was it, if I had died, it wouldn't have been any different to how things unfolded. It was a sad epiphany.

I sincerely hope that you, as the reader, never have to experience such an extreme event before realising that there is more to life than this. Open your eyes and see that there are alternative ways to live.

You are not afraid to be judged

I assume you are not afraid to be judge by other people around you, your friends, families, and society. Being a nomad and an entrepreneur involves going against the grain, they have a saying that when starting off in business it is always your family that are the last to believe you, but the first ones at the table when you succeed. Everyone is always skeptical about the business venture you are starting, and warn you about potential losses and constantly encourage you to go back to being to the safe employee, rarely do we hear entrepreneurs or even just mavericks get supported by their families at the beginning unless they themselves were entrepreneurs to begin with.

Professional Gamers when starting off their parents are constantly nagging on them about how they are wasting their life playing video games all the time until they win millions dollars cash price in a tournament then suddenly they become the doting parents that has always believed in their kids.

Professional NBA players, Actors, Youtube Stars, Streamers, Entrepreneurs and anything unorthodox to the employee blueprint almost always will face questioning by friends, families and their communities, and for good reason, it is a complete black box to them, what they think is a gamble on life they cannot imagine.

The same individuals who judge us often are the ones who are not afraid to work diligently and put their head down for 32 years.

Now, let's consider the traditional. If you had worked for 32 years in a corporate job, there would be no chance for a serendipitous event to change your fortune. Year after year, you would continue working tirelessly, with only small increases in income – perhaps around 5% per annum – just enough to keep up with inflation. By the time you retire, your golden nest egg would only afford you an ordinary life similar to how you are living now, a live to work mindset.

It's important to acknowledge that when you first embark on this journey as a nomad entrepreneur, people will judge you and treat you as a maverick. They may doubt your abilities or question your choices. But here's the thing: that judgment is temporary. It will only last until the day when you prove them wrong. That day could come sooner than expected – perhaps within a week or a month – or it could also take years of relentless effort and perseverance. That's the beauty of it all – the unknown, the uncertainty of what lies ahead rather than settling for a 'guaranteed' bare minimum life in three decades.

You are patient

I assume you know the value of patience. Unlike normal jobs where income and growth are linear, being an entrepreneur the potential returns are asymmetrical, you could see zero income and zero growth for months on end and finally one day it becomes worth $10 million dollars. You see it all the time, even in talent shows, when someone has been grinding behind the scenes for years, only to be discovered by someone who sees their potential. And the next minute, they are catapulted into stardom.

We've seen this skyrocketing multiple times before, seemingly nobodies just streaming their daily lives or their dance moves one minute then the next day becomes household names. Before their tipping point event, every one of them they were just quietly bidding their time, being judge by their friends, families and society, imagine telling *Ed Sheeran* stop playing guitar at random places and just get a corporate job.

The same goes for businesses, startups founder earn barely enough week on week at the beginning, until they get funded or their products take off, we've seen it multiple times in big tech companies like Facebook, Amazon, Uber, and more recently OpenAI. OpenAI seemingly just came out of nowhere and has become a household name that is threatening jobs everywhere.

These are more household names that may seem too far out of reach, but it's worth taking the time to research the entrepreneurs who quietly earn thousands of dollars a day. They could be the seemingly ordinary neighbour you see at the local coffee shop, taking his time to enjoy his coffee, dressed in ordinary clothes and not rushing for that 9 am meeting. They have full control of their time taking enjoying their mornings. Society made us believe that all millionaires and entrepreneurs live luxurious lives, wearing fancy clothes and driving fancy cars. But true luxury is time; having control of what we want to do when we want to do it, without having the fear of not having food on the table or not being able to provide for our families.

Consider the average software engineer who built a website once to solve a specific problem and now rakes in profits while lounging around in Bali Indonesia. Think about the people who capitalised on the Dot Com boom, AI boom, Cryptocurrency boom, NFT boom - all of whom are now set for life and don't have to work a day in their lives. They were patient and took action when opportunities presented themselves.

You have to be willing to weather the storm of judgement if you want to join these group of people who seemingly have cracked the code to life, because that's all you have, if you think about what is the alternative really? Being patient and keeping your head down working for 32 years and hope for at least a million dollars at the end? The average money people have saved after retirement is around $200,000.

Again, 32 years, average career length for $200k, average retirement savings. Let that sink in for a bit.

You are hungry

I assume you are in your prime ages or about to enter the best years of your life, how you interpret what the best years of your life is up to you.

A significant portion of the wisdom in this book revolves around experimenting and figuring things out, which requires dedication and effort. If you have become jaded and have given up on trying, I cannot make that mind shift for you. It must come from within. Your desire for success should extend beyond yourself to providing for you and your family for generations to come, rather than being content to work hard for 32 years only to retire with barely enough.

Your desire should be strong enough to drive you to want to visit the Eiffel Tower and create beautiful memories with your life partner while you still can. You shouldn't find yourself barely staying awake during a Gondola Ride in Venice while the boat's driver earns your hard-earned cash because you've given the prime of your life working for someone else.

Let's Get Started

Before we continue, I want to emphasise that these are not rigid boundaries, but rather flexible guidelines or signposts. They provide a glimpse into what the book is about and give you a sense of its tone before delving into the intricacies of what it truly entails. I hate wasting time, and this section allows you to not waste your time reading a book that is possibly not your cup of tea, you could see yourself as a complete opposite or think that there is no value further pursuing reading this book.

It's important to note that you don't have to fit all of the criteria mentioned above in order to read this book. Even if you fear being judged by others or if you've never experienced corporate life but deep down know it's not for you, that doesn't diminish the valuable lessons and strategies you can gain from reading this book.

If the above still makes sense for you and you are still here, thinking, "I can relate to one or more of these criteria" and have been pondering if there's more to life than what you currently have, then let us continue on our journey together. Let's explore what it truly takes to transform your life into one that is more fulfilling and satisfying.

Types of Digital Nomads

"The world is a book, and those who do not travel read only a page." - Saint Augustine

You might have gathered from the title and the table of contents of this book what kind of digital nomad I am and what we will discussing in this book, but I wanted to be explicit on all other different types of nomads out there and why we are focusing on just one.

Types of Nomads:

- Armchair Nomads
- Experimental Nomads
- Salaried Nomads
- Freelance Nomads
- Entrepreneur Nomads

Armchair Nomads

Armchair Nomads is often the entry point or gateway to the lifestyle. It serves as the starting point for every aspiring nomad's journey. The spectrum of individuals interested in this lifestyle varies, from those who do a little bit of research online and read about it from others, to those who daydream about it incessantly. However, there is always just one thing that stops them from taking the leap and fully committing to this way of life. This obstacle could take on various forms:

- Financial constraints
- Current responsibilities
- Lack of support from spouses or partners
- Waiting for children to reach a suitable age
- Insufficient skills to work remotely
- Employers prohibiting remote work
- Passport or country restrictions

Being on the armchair could either be the end journey or the beginning of it. Those who never pull the trigger will always have another obstacle, event, or excuse that will always get in the way. The truth is, circumstances rarely align perfectly and life often throws unexpected challenges our way. It is incredibly rare for everything to fall into place and become easy for us to uproot and leave without any difficulties. When the kids leave the nest, you have health issues already. When you've saved enough money, you've already committed to a mortgage. If you don't prioritise making change, something will always get in the way and it will never happen.

I was born in a third-world country, with arguably one of the least privileged passport in Southeast Asia. Normally, when traveling overseas, I would always have to produce a mountain of paperwork just to prove that I wasn't attempting to stay illegally in any country. I always had to provide proof of employment, including employment contracts and payslips, just to prove that I wasn't going to stay long-term. Whenever I needed to go to more developed countries, I needed to know someone who already lived there and vouched for me that they also knew me, they would need to write a letter to an embassy that states if something were to happen they were willing to cover my expenses. Only then would the embassies even consider granting me a visa. This was all just so I can travel for a couple of days, it felt like the odds were always against me.

Some would say that having a weak passport is a key detriment to the nomadic lifestyle, causing them to give up on the idea altogether. I've committed so much time and energy in figuring out how to make it possible, doing countless research to better understand what are all my options to be able to obtain a stronger passport. Now that I do have a stronger passport, it enables me to move freely to different countries with relatively more ease than before, I still fondly look back from time to time at all the trials that I had to go through just to fly out my own country.

Early on in my life I was part of this group, the Armchair Nomads, I was constantly telling my friends, "I'll do it, I'll quit my job and travel the world with only a couple of suitcases in tow." I kept saying and but never committing to doing it. When I was finally faced with a series of traumatic life events, I had to take a long look at my life and asked myself what is it I truly want out of my life. This introspection was the final catalyst to make the decision to make the jump from Armchair Nomad to actually becoming one.

Once I've made the commitment internally, it didn't matter what my circumstance was, I made the sacrifices and the rest was history.

My aim for this book is to empower you to make the necessary decisions: either to get of the armchair and live your best life, or accept the harsh reality that it will never happen. Whichever path you choose, my goal is to provide you with all the information you need about the lifestyle, both the positives and negatives. Because in the end, indecisiveness and not doing anything is much worst than trying and failing.

Experimental Nomads

Experimental nomads are the ones a bit more courageous than the armchair, they take an extended vacation or long unpaid leave off work to travel the world but in the long-run still comes back to being a corporate worker.

If you've met an experimental nomad that have had to come back to a corporate setting, they are much different than they were before they left. They will say they are actively just saving up for the next opportunity to make the jump again. You can also see it in their eyes, their spirit is never fully back. They are still day dreaming about the lifestyle they enjoyed while traveling the world, seeing the beautiful scenery of different parts of the world, and meeting interesting people. Most importantly, they reminisce about the freedom they had, not having to be somewhere reporting to someone.

The experimental nomads just comes back to their 9-5 job only to save enough money to one day plan again to travel without having the need to be forced back to the corporate world, they haven't cracked the code and figured out how to sustain the lifestyle, they haven't burned their boats and always cling to the idea of a 'stable' job, hence they never truly unlock what it is to being a nomad and attaining true freedom. What they don't know is that they are getting the short end of the stick; paying for both lifestyles while spending the majority of the time on the corporate ladder, they wonder how these digital nomads sustain such lifestyles of constantly traveling the world. Their fear of going all-in becomes much more unsustainable in the long run.

What is the expression: "Burn your boat?"

The story of burning your boats is a metaphorical tale that originates from the famous Spanish conquistador, Hernán Cortés. It is said that in the early 16th century, Cortés and his men arrived in Mexico with the intention of conquering the powerful Aztec empire.

Legend has it that upon arrival, Cortés ordered his men to burn their boats, thus leaving them with no option but to fight and conquer or die. By eliminating any possibility of retreat or surrender, Cortés was able to instill a sense of urgency and determination in his troops. They were left with no choice but to face their enemy head-on, as there was no way back home.

This act of burning the boats symbolised a commitment to success at all costs. It represented a complete dedication to achieving their goal, even in the face of immense challenges and a seemingly impossible mission. With no alternative but victory, Cortés and his men fought fiercely against the Aztecs and eventually succeeded in overthrowing their empire.

The story of burning your boats has since become a popular metaphor for total commitment and taking bold action towards achieving one's goals. It signifies a mindset where there is no turning back or giving up. By eliminating all other options, individuals are forced to confront challenges head-on and push themselves beyond their limits in pursuit of success.

Salaried Nomads

Salaried Nomads, in my opinion, are the worst of both worlds and unfortunately, they make up the majority of nomads.

This lifestyle is essentially a life hack where you get paid from first-world countries but live in a country that gives you more buying power, instantly tripling the value of your money. Any job that doesn't require you to be physically in an office can achieve this lifestyle, but the caveat is it is dependent on whether your employer allows you to work anywhere or if you are willing to find ingenious ways of making your employer believe you are still on the same state.

Think about it for a moment. You're a rational and mature person, yet you have to ask permission from someone else if you want to live somewhere else and still be able to provide for yourself and your family. This dynamic often belittles the value you produce for your company. Why should I need permission to work where I want if I can still get the job done? The traditional way of thinking is that work and value mean being physically present in an office, but this is outdated. If the COVID pandemic has proven anything, is that most businesses can operate as usual without employees being physically there, specifically knowledge-based businesses.

This is one of the main reasons why I believe being a Salaried Nomad is the worst of both worlds. Essentially, you are still at the mercy of an employer while living in possibly both different time zones and less optimal conditions. I do not see a lot of Salaried Nomads living in five-star hotels nor do I see them having ergonomic desk setup that they can bring anywhere, they are either in shared hostels or staying in longer-term house rentals without proper office equipment. Often, Salaried Nomads choose cheaper countries, which can result in less than ideal living scenarios, yet the expectations from their work remains the same if not more because they have the privilege to work remote.

Imagine being in a tropical country in Asia where the workday starts at 8pm because you work for a company in the other side of the world. You have no choice but to adjust to their schedule. And when it comes time to travel from one location to another (which will inevitably happen), you always have to play catch-up because time was lost from the employer's perspective. The work never stops regardless of what you have going on in your personal life or how long it takes for you to adjust to a new place.

In addition, high-speed internet isn't available everywhere you go. How can you attend meetings when you keep getting disconnected? And what will your boss think if they see the beach behind you during a meeting? It's unlikely that you'll be wearing your swimsuit to a corporate meeting, so do you wear office attire at the beach or cafe? Additionally, there are no chargers on the beach, cafes can be too loud for productivity, and internet speed may prevent any semblance of getting work done. Unless, the work you do is completely asynchronous the simple logistics becomes tricky to implement in the day to day.

While it is still feasible, the sheer inconvenience of trying to sustain corporate work outdoors will likely lead you to working in co-working spaces or dedicated working stations within hostels, BnBs, and hotels. I've seen many digital nomads toiling away at these spaces without proper chairs, monitors, or equipment necessary for their jobs. It's not what they expected. Imagine spending the whole day hunched over a substandard desk, working solely on your laptop screen for more than 8 hours because bringing your office chair or big monitors with you isn't possible. Everyone has their own makeshift portable workstation setups like foldable origami stands for their laptops. But at the end of the day, it's far from ideal or sustainable for office work. You end up with poor working conditions and are unable to truly enjoy what each place has to offer. And the feeling of dread and thoughts of "this is not what I signed up for" start to sink in.

The counterargument often heard is that, as a digital nomad, "I can work by the beach or in a chic cafe while others are stuck in the office, and my money goes much further." Give it some further thought, do you really think the owner of the cafe doesn't mind you staying for more than a couple of hours at a time? How about 8 hours? Do you think you can come in day in and day out for the majority of the week without no one bothering you while you are in a meeting? More often than not the trouble is more than it's worth. It becomes then staying mostly indoors for most of the work day, which may be completely different from the life you had envisioned being a digital nomad or how social media portrays the lifestyle to be. It's up to you to weigh those factors personally when you're in it. I've seen people go back to the office and their home country after giving it a try for a couple of months.

Instead of trying to do both – being a digital nomad and an employee – it would be better to commit fully to being a nomad entrepreneur and earning while you sleep. Trying to balance both worlds won't live up to what you see on social media; instead, it will likely result in getting stuck in a co-working space with other employees who are also working for different companies. It'll be exactly the same as your office back home, but with added hassle and isolation.

This is not to pass judgement on Salaried Nomads, not everyone can be entrepreneurs, and not everyone is unhappy about working 9-5 jobs. The point I make is that if you were to make an active choice of which one you should pursue, wouldn't you want to take control of your time and be your own boss. You owe it to yourself.

Freelance Nomad

Freelance Nomads, are in a way a step above the salaried ones, not necessarily by how much they earn but they've embraced the lifestyle and are honing their craft to be their own bosses, they get clients and are starting to build their names and their brands. They have full control of their time but their income is currently directly tied to clients and value they deliver.

There are various types of freelance jobs, such as logo design, copyright writing, software development, and much more. These digital nomads are highly adaptable and accustomed to the unpredictable nature of their lifestyle. They don't rely on a fixed monthly salary to make ends meet and are one step closer to ultimate freedom.

Currently, they are learning how to scale their work and achieve the same results with less effort. They have mastered the art of decoupling time and effort from their work. For instance, a web designer can create different templates for different types of requests. When they receive a new customer who needs a website for a restaurant, they can simply make minor tweaks to an existing template used for another restaurant. This way, they can sell the website for the same price but with less effort involved. Over time, as their collection of assets grows, they can gradually reduce their working hours while increasing their income. Their reputation as the go-to freelancer also helps in attracting more clients.

By leveraging their technical skills and effectively communicating with clients, these freelancers have been able to successfully navigate the freelance market and establish themselves as leaders in their respective fields, allowing them to live the lifestyle they choose.

Entrepreneur Nomad

The Entrepreneur Nomad, the pinnacle of nomads, is the epitome of freedom and success in the digital age. Unlike traditional workers, they do not equate their time to money earned. Instead, they focus on creating assets that generate passive income. For example, or creating a online masterclass that can provide continuous earnings for years to come. They understand the power of "build once, earn multiple times."

This lifestyle may seem like a distant dream for many, but it is indeed possible. In the finance section of this book, we will explore the mindset shift required to achieve this level of success. As you read along, I will share stories and experiences from individuals who have already done it, inspiring you and showing you what is truly within the realm of possibility. A simple case study is "Design Joy," it's company run by a solo designer, which earns 1 million dollars a year by offering design as a subscription model. Charging clients more than 5 grand per client, instead of compelling them to hire full-time designers, they leverage the owner's expertise in the design world through his own reusable assets.

Believe it or not, there are already people out there earning over $100k *per month* without being tied to corporate jobs or working long hours. The digital nomad entrepreneur knows how to leverage what each country has to offer in order to get ahead financially. They become tax residents in countries with favourable tax laws, invest in prime real estate around the world, and embrace the true essence of being a citizen of the world.

This lifestyle is incredibly rewarding but also incredibly challenging. It requires determination, resilience, and a strong heart. It's not for everyone, but for those who are willing to take the leap of faith, it can be truly life-changing.

This is what Golden Visa is all about – Access to a world of unlimited possibilities.

In this book, we will delve deep into the life of a global nomad entrepreneur and uncover what it takes to crack the code of life on your own terms. We will explore the mindset you need to cultivate for success, how to manage your finances so that you can focus on your journey without constant worry, and what you can expect along the way – both highs and lows. Lastly, we will discuss the core competencies that will aid you in your journey to attaining your own Golden Visa, helping you become a successful nomad entrepreneur.

Chapter Summary: Types of Digital Nomads

- There are different types of nomads, including armchair nomads, experimental nomads, salaried nomads, freelance nomads, and entrepreneur nomads.
- Armchair nomads are interested in the lifestyle but face obstacles like financial constraints or lack of support from partners.
- Experimental nomads take extended vacations but often return to corporate jobs without fully achieving the freedom they desire.
- Burning your boats is a metaphor for committing fully to a goal with no possibility of retreat or surrender.
- Salaried nomads live in cheaper countries but still work for employers and face challenges like time zone differences and lack of proper work conditions.
- Freelance nomads have more control over their time and income as they work for clients and are starting to build their brands.
- Entrepreneur nomads focus on creating assets that generate passive income and enjoy ultimate freedom and success.
- This book focuses on becoming an Entrepreneur nomad and ultimately attaining the 'Golden Visa', access to a world of unlimited possibility.

Part 1: MINDSET

Two-Luggage Constraint and Minimalism

"The things you own end up owning you." - Tyler Durden (Fight Club)

It's difficult to discuss digital nomadism without first connecting it to minimalism. In fact, it seems that being a minimalist is almost a prerequisite for being a digital nomad because of the physical constraints of traveling around the world. But what exactly is minimalism? According to a quick Google search, minimalism "promotes conscious decision-making about belongings, time, energy, and relationships." *Joshua Fields Millburn and Ryan Nicodemus*, Emmy-nominated Netflix stars, podcasters, and New York Times–bestselling authors, define it as a tool that can help you find freedom.

Different people interpret minimalism differently based on their stage in life. Some equate it with having as little as possible to minimise their spending and material attachments. Others view it as a way to minimise waste as much as they can. And then there are those who see it as synonymous with freedom—whatever form that may take. There is no definitive meaning of minimalism; rather, you have the freedom to define what minimalism means to you. The only commonality is that it does not rely on material things to be the source of your happiness. While there are certainly blueprints and guidelines available, no one will enforce certain rules or give you a stamp of approval. You have the power to decide what aspects of your life you want to minimise in order to maximise joy in your daily life.

Concrete Jungle in Tow

When we apply the concept of minimalism to digital nomadism, there are obvious constraints in the form of luggage and suitcases. Simply put, it's impossible for someone to bring an entire house with them while traveling the world—unless you happen to be *Dwayne "The Rock" Johnson* who frequently brings his own gym wherever he goes in order to stay grounded. There is nothing inherently wrong with wanting to bring your entire life along with you on your nomadic journey; however, like anything else in life, there is a cost associated with it, usually in the form of monetary and mental clutter that it takes up.

Bringing all of your belongings with you as you travel the world doesn't necessarily add much value in the grand scheme of things. Just think about it: Do you really need to bring your 55-inch television with you wherever you go? Technically, you could, but why would you want to? Additionally, airport regulations and country restrictions may prevent you from bringing certain items with you. Ideally, the only things that should be in your luggage are the essentials.

This first step of letting go of most of your possessions can be a major hurdle for many people and often serves as the reason why they never take the leap into becoming a nomad—even though most people dream about becoming one. The sooner we realise and accept that clinging on to our material possessions is holding us back from a life of freedom, the sooner it is we start to take steps to let them go. The first step is always being mindful of the problem we want to have a solution to. It doesn't necessarily mean we start selling all our things right this instant, it could mean taking mental steps to let go and not have strong dependencies on them. It means just being okay with the fact that you could survive without all the daily comfort you are so accustomed to in your day to day life.

Loss Aversion

We have a natural inclination to hold on to things and feel the pain of loss twice as deeply. This cognitive bias is known as Loss Aversion. It's a psychological quirk that we often experience when it comes to money—we feel double the pain when we lose $100 compared to the positive feeling of gaining $100 for free. To counterbalance that feeling of loss, we would need to gain twice as much as what we lost—for example, we need to gain $200 to compensate for the feeling of losing $100, just ask someone who's played one too many hand in the casino, and it starts to make sense why it's easy to spiral down into crippling debt.

But loss aversion isn't limited to money; it also applies to the idea of letting go of 90% of our belongings or storing them away. We hesitate to sell our shirts at garage sales, even if we haven't worn them in years, or even decades. Yes, Sentimentality is deeply ingrained in our nature, but maybe we are also just heavily influenced by Loss Aversion; that the thought of letting go of things we don't need feels a lot more like losing something rather gaining more mental space.

Regardless, understanding this aspect of human psychology is crucial before considering a nomadic lifestyle. If we are unable to understand what holds us back from letting go of things that we hold on to we will never make the leap, and the freedom and flexibility that come with a nomadic lifestyle will always be out of reach. It's not just about physical belongings either; it's also about the emotional attachments we have to certain places, relationships, and routines. We cling to familiarity and find comfort in the known, even if it means sacrificing our desire for adventure and growth.

But here's the thing: letting go doesn't have to be a painful experience. In fact, it can be incredibly liberating. By shedding the weight of unnecessary possessions and attachments, we create space for new experiences and opportunities to enter our lives. We open ourselves up to a world of possibilities that wouldn't have been available had we stayed trapped in our comfort zones.

Think about it this way: every item we own requires time, energy, and mental space to maintain. The more things we accumulate, the more cluttered our lives become. This clutter not only occupies physical space but also weighs us down mentally and emotionally. It becomes a burden that hinders our ability to focus on what truly matters.

Psychologist Barry Schwartz, did a study on what they call "the paradox of choice" which means simply put having too many options can lead to decision fatigue. Imagine having a closet of a thousand dresses, and you have been invited to attend Saturday's BBQ at your neighbours house. The mental space it takes to go through each dress and figure out what to wear could take seconds, minutes, or hours for you to decide, and by the time you have decided you aren't even sure if the dress you picked is the best one for the occasion. Having too many options is sometimes a bad thing. Rather than focusing on connecting and getting to know your neighbours more, you have been too cluttered with simply what to wear. Now, this could be an exaggeration of a decision on what to wear, but imagine having all those tiny decision multiplied throughout the day. Which shoe am I going to wear, which bag am I going to bring, which book am I going to read, which show am I going to watch, and on and on we go.

By embracing minimalism and practicing intentional living, we can break free from the chains of decision fatigue and loss aversion. We can then begin to reclaim control over our lives and focus on things that truly matter. We can learn to distinguish between what is truly valuable to us and what is merely holding us back. It's about shifting our mindset from one of scarcity and fear of loss to one of abundance and freedom.

So how do we start? Begin by taking inventory of your belongings — both physical and emotional — and ask yourself what truly adds value to your life. Be ruthless in decluttering your physical space, letting go of items that no longer serve a purpose or bring you joy. What are things that are truly worth holding onto versus what are things that I keep because of familiarity.

Remember, letting go is not synonymous with giving up or losing something; it's about making room for something better. It's about creating space for growth, change, and new opportunities. So take the leap, embrace the unknown, and trust that the universe will fill the void with something extraordinary. And when you do, you'll realise that the pain of letting go is nothing compared to the joy of living a life without limits.

Chapter Summary: Two-Luggage Constraint and Minimalism

- Minimalism is an implicit requirement to travel due to the physical constraints of our luggages and suitcases.
- Minimalism promotes conscious decision-making about belongings, time, energy, and relationships .
- Different people have different interpretations of minimalism.
- Loss aversion is a cognitive bias that makes it difficult for us to let go of things and understanding it is crucial before considering a nomadic lifestyle.
- Bringing unnecessary belongings while traveling adds monetary and mental clutter.
- Letting go of possessions can be a major hurdle for many people who dream of becoming nomads.
- Letting go can be liberating and create space for new experiences and opportunities.
- Embracing minimalism helps break free from loss aversion and regain control over our lives.

Purpose Driven Buys

"The price of anything is the amount of life you exchange for it." - Henry David Thoreau

Do you ever find yourself tempted to buy things simply because they're on sale, only to later regret your purchase? Or do you view buying things as a way to show off your status or measure your success? Before we delve deeper into this topic, let me clarify that I'm not suggesting you become incredibly frugal or cheap. In his book "*I Will Teach You to Be Rich*," *Ramit Sethi* advises defining what truly brings you happiness and what you genuinely want to spend money on. Splurge on those things, but scrutinise everything else and be extra diligent. It's never been about denying yourself and not getting the things you want, if buying coffee from the cafe helps you jumpstart the day and brings joy in your life, then by all means, buy that coffee. Don't let people on the internet tell you that pinching pennies is the way to go. It's about being deliberate about it though, it's making the choices about what truly brings you joy and adds value to you.

It's interesting to note that many millionaires are frugal in some areas of their lives while being extravagant in others. For example, Warren Buffet still drives the same car he had before he became wealthy but spends millions of dollars in his investments. Elon Musk when he initially sold PayPal, spent all his money to start SpaceX and had to borrow money from his friends to cover his daily expenditure. This is because people who understand the value of purposeful spending are willing to spend without hesitation on things they know will add value and bring them happiness, while being frugal with everything else.

80-20 Rule

If we apply the *Pareto Principle (also known as the 80-20 rule)*, only a small portion of our belongings (about 20%) is truly worth spending money on, yet these possessions bring us most of the outcomes we desire (about 80%). When we aren't mindful about our spending choices, we end up wasting money on things that hold no real value for us. Coupled with our cognitive bias towards *Loss Aversion*, this can lead us to hoard unnecessary items and even buy larger houses just to store them. As Chuck Palahniuk wrote in *Fight Club*, "We buy things we don't need with money we don't have to impress people we don't like."

As a software engineer myself, I don't hesitate to invest in a high-quality laptop that costs several thousand dollars because it directly impacts my craft and enables me to write code or books effectively. Similarly, I don't think twice about buying healthy food, even if it may be more expensive than regular or unhealthy options. To me, if I'm don't feel healthy, everything else becomes meaningless.

What non-negotiable for me may not be the same for you, you could be someone who doesn't need a high-end computer for their day to day life. Or you do. That's the beauty of it all, every one has their own unique set of essentials, you need to figure out what those are and stick ruthlessly to it.

10 Million Dollar Question

There is a viral video on YouTube where one person asks another, "If I give you ten million dollars, would you take it?" The obvious answer is yes. But then the follow-up question is asked, "Would you take it if you wouldn't wake up tomorrow?" This prompts us to reflect on how the ability to live and wake up each day holds more value than any amount of money in the world. Unfortunately, there are people who take this for granted. I've encountered business associates from well-known companies who are extremely frugal when it comes to food but don't hesitate to spend money on expensive clothing. They fail to invest in their personal growth.

Things That Own You

I have a close friend who has always been obsessed with big-name brands and constantly craved the next new thing. At one point, I was traveling the world and happened to be visiting the country he was in.

Out of nowhere, he sent me a message asking about a plain yellow shirt from a specific brand that he wanted as a gift. The shirt itself appeared ordinary and reasonably durable, but I couldn't fathom why it would cost over $500. However, my friend insisted that this was the only shirt he wanted. It didn't matter if I had bought him any other yellow shirt; he would have been utterly disappointed as if something had gone wrong. In addition to this incident, he had asked me to buy various items for him in the past—always requesting specific brands without considering any aesthetic or practical aspects of those items.

He would travel with all his belongings packed into expensive luggage and take photos of them everywhere he went, as if these material possessions had lives of their own and were traveling alongside him. He constantly stressed about leaving his possessions in hotel rooms, triple-checked that he had locked them away, and avoided staying out for too long or taking his things with him to prevent theft.

The worst part was when he flew overseas and had to check in his luggage, being far away from his belongings caused him constant distress during the flight, worrying whether his luggage would arrive safely at his destination.

My friend lies on the extreme end of the spectrum when it comes to material possessions, but it's clear that these things have ended up owning him. They have taken on a life of their own, constantly gnawing at the back of his mind.

Let Go And Grow

Becoming a digital nomad or preparing to become one requires a shift in mindset. It's not about being excessively frugal or buying low-cost material items while surviving on instant noodles for the rest of your life in a developing country. That is no way to truly live. Instead, it's about understanding yourself and identifying the things that bring genuine value and meaning to your life. It's about being disciplined enough to let go of things that don't add value.

On our travels around the world, we always ensure that there are high quality supermarkets nearby so we can get access to fresh fruits and vegetables. We also put having a walkable area nearby as one of our main criteria in deciding where to say. We, me and my wife, find that to be able to talk while having long walks in the morning has become one of our non-negotiable and it helps us jump start and energise us throughout our day.

Having a clearer understanding of what is critical versus what is not empowers you then to make decisions and compromises to live a sustainable life. I don't need to stay in five-star luxury hotels if I can have a access to good food and walkable areas. Without having a clearer understanding of what is truly important to you, trade-offs become happenstance, and you are easily swayed by external factors, such as quick sales and price drops, which in the long run do not truly bring joy to your life.

Action Point: Take a moment to look around your home and assess your belongings. Are there items you hold onto simply because you're afraid of losing them? Take stock of all your possessions and consider what truly adds value to your life

---

Chapter Summary:Purpose-Driven Buys

- The Pareto Principle (80-20 rule) applies to spending, with only a small portion of belongings being worth spending money on.
- Hoarding unnecessary items and buying larger houses to store them is a common consequence of mindless spending.
- Investing in high-quality tools or items that directly impact one's craft or well-being is justified.
- The value of waking up each day holds more importance than any amount of money.
- Material possessions can end up owning people and causing constant stress and anxiety.
- Becoming a digital nomad requires a shift in mindset, focusing on things that bring genuine value and meaning to life.
- Letting go of things that don't add value is essential for personal growth and fulfilment.
- Take stock of all possessions and consider what truly adds value to life.

Dealing with Fear

"Courage is not the absence of fear, but rather the assessment that
something else is more important than fear." - Franklin D. Roosevelt

No lifestyle comes without a price, for any way you live your life
comes with its consequences and associated fears. A single person might
fear being alone for the rest of their life, an elderly person might fear
getting into an accident and being unable to call for help, an employee
might fear losing their job, a wealthy person might fear damaging their
reputation, a parent might fear how their children will grow up in the

current state of the economy, and an obese person might fear for their future health if they do not change their lifestyle.

Napoleon Hill from the book *"Think And Grow Rich"* identifies six primal fears that everyone shares. He argues that all forms of fears at their core can be attributed to one of these six:

- Fear of poverty
- Fear of criticism
- Fear of poor health
- Fear of loss of loved ones
- Fear of old age
- Fear of death

Public Speaking and Death

This is why some people fear public speaking so much that they would literally rather die than speak in public. A group of psychologists studied a group of people and ranked how much they feared public speaking and dying. Surprisingly, the number of people who would rather die than speak in public was surprisingly high.

"At a funeral, the average person would rather be in the casket than giving the eulogy." –Jerry Seinfeld

Each one of us has primal fears that outweigh other fears. Some people fear criticism more than death and would rather die than speak in public. Some people are driven by their fear of poverty and will never consider leaving a secure job even if it means sacrificing time with family (loss of loved ones). This is something intrinsic to how each one of us operates.

There are ways for people to overcome such fears, but the key to considering a life of global lifestyle is first understanding what your primal fears are. Do you crave stability (fear of poverty)? Do you fear failure (fear of criticism)? Do you fear a life not well-lived (fear of old age)?

Personally, my primal fear was poverty, so even the thought of jumping into the unknown and pursuing an entrepreneurial life was not something I thought I would pursue. I would rather speak in public than give up my job!

What is your Primal Fear?

Take the time to reflect and understand what your main fears are. If a nomad life is something you want to pursue, then you need to understand what you fear the most. Why is this important? Because when things get tough and uncertain, which nomadic/entrepreneurial lifestyles inevitably bring, you need to be grounded in understanding who you are and what you are afraid of. Hopefully, by that time, it will be more manageable because you've done the work and wrestled with the demons in your head.

Sometimes, mentally preparing yourself for what could happen is an exercise in itself. That way, you won't be as shocked when faced with challenging situations. *Tim Ferris*, the author of *The 4-Hour Workweek,* does an interesting exercise called 'Fear-Setting'. It's a process where he lists down all his absolute worst fears in one column and writes down what he would do if those scenarios actually happened in another column. More often than not, he realises that it wasn't as bad as he thought and that he would still be fine even if the absolute worst were to happen.

Action Point: Pause and reflect. What is your primal fear? How would you deal with it if your worst fears came true? Is this something you can do something about? Do your 'Fear-Setting' exercise - write down all your absolute fears and how you would deal with them if they were to happen.

Dry-Run Nomad

The good news is there are several ways to practice being a digital nomad before making the full-time commitment. However, I do want to warn you that regardless of how many of these you try, it will never be the same as when you actually make the change. These activities give you a glimpse of how the lifestyle would be, but nothing will fully prepare you for the jump. It's like speaking on stage - no matter how long you practice in front of a mirror or an empty stage, you never foresee how your brain reacts when there are hundreds or thousands of people in front of you. No matter how well practiced and memorised your speech is, the actual experience can be different.

Nonetheless, below is a list of activities that can give you a glimpse and at least provide you head-start on how things will be in this lifestyle:

- Going on an extended unpaid vacation
- Changing jobs frequently
- Relocating to another country
- Staying in hotels for more than a week, even in non-touristy areas
- Engaging in long-term camping
- Embarking on a cross-country RV journey

- Being unemployed for 2-3 months
- Generating income outside of employment
- Starting a side-hustle
- Trying out freelancing

Each activity/event has elements of both positivity and negativity in terms of how life would be as a nomad. I advise you to try at least 2-3 events from the list to mentally prepare yourself. If I had to recommend my top 3 choices, they would be:

- Having no job for 2-3 months
- Going on a cross-country RV trip
- Camping for an extended period of time.

Take a Break

Having no job, especially for overachievers who have always been able to find jobs instantly or for those who wouldn't dare leave their job until another one is already lined up, can be eye-opening. I've met people who have had their last day of work on a Friday only to start another the following Monday, perfectly aligning their contracts so they don't have any downtime. This is counter-intuitive and does not give you space to reflect.

Not giving yourself any room to meditate and reflect on the previous job and not taking the time to recover and figure out what went wrong is the fastest way to being trapped in the rat-race mentality. When you consciously choose not to look for another job for 2-3 months, and the initial adrenaline of leaving your previous job subsides, your mind starts to wander. You become itchy and busy as you were constantly under pressure from Monday to Friday, only to then have so much quiet time. This could be shocking for an employee, but you will learn a lot about yourself when you decide to just be still and get comfortable with being uncomfortable. You'll go through your mental backlog of what you wanted to do when you were younger and a bit more naive. Do you even remember that feeling when you had big dreams and all these plans of grandeur until life happened and you signed away your freedom?

Another activity is camping or staying in a van for an extended period of time. The limitation of packing only the things you need in a van or campsite forces you to reassess how much clutter you have accumulated over the years and realise how much you don't really need to enjoy life. It can be especially uncomfortable if you've never done such activities, but that's the whole point - putting yourself out of your comfort zone and spending more time with yourself doing something you truly want versus just dreaming about it without a concrete plan. This activity is especially powerful when go completely offline during your trip and immersed yourself completely in nature.

Personally, I have done all of the activities on the list. I have moved countries three times, lived in different states, worked for 10 companies, lived in a van for a period of time, lived in hotels for a period of time - overall practicing being a nomad, I didn't know it back then that this was going to be my path moving forward. So when I actually became a nomad after packing all our things and putting them in storage, saying goodbye to our friends and families, and telling them we were traveling the world, we didn't experience too much shock from the difference in lifestyle because we were already living our lives that way. Although it was still quite different from the dry-runs, it didn't feel like jumping into ice-cold water, but more like gradually dropping into freezing water after experiencing a drop in temperature.

Action Point: Choose 3 activities/events from the list above and make them happen in your life, whether it's earning money outside of work or taking an extended vacation. Pick what is feasible given your circumstances. After each event, do a retrospective and assess how it felt. What did you like about it? What made you uncomfortable? Reflect on whether these things are something you can manage in exchange for a life of freedom. Did the positive aspects outweigh the negative? This is a good checkpoint to see if being a nomad is something you would actually enjoy or if you just like the idea of it.

Chapter Summary: Dealing with Fear

- Fear of poverty, criticism, poor health, loss of loved ones, old age, and death are identified as primal fears.

- Some people fear public speaking more than death, understanding your primal fears is important before considering a global lifestyle.

- Tim Ferris recommends doing a "Fear-Setting" exercise to confront worst fears, reflect and understand your main fears and how you would deal with them if they came true.

- There are ways to practice being a digital nomad before fully committing to the lifestyle. Trying activities like extended unpaid vacation, changing jobs frequently, or relocating to another country can provide a glimpse into nomad life.

- Taking a break from work for 2-3 months can be eye-opening and help reflect on your purpose.

Avoid the Rat Race by Knowing What is Enough

"The greatest wealth is to live content with little." - Plato

There is an old proverb about a fisherman and a businessman, and the story goes like this:

The Parable of the Fisherman

A businessman visits a small fishing village and sees a fisherman returning to shore with his catch. The fisherman had been out fishing since early morning and had caught enough fish to support his family. Intrigued, the businessman approaches the fisherman and tells him that if he were to fish longer, he could catch more fish, sell them, and make more money. The fisherman asks why he would need to do that.

The businessman explains that with more money, the fisherman could buy a bigger boat, hire some employees, and expand his business.

Eventually, the businessman says, the fisherman could even move to a big city and become very successful. At this point, the fisherman asks what he would do once he becomes successful.

The businessman responds by saying that he would then be able to spend more time with his family, relax on the beach, and enjoy life. The irony of the story is revealed when the fisherman tells the businessman that he is already doing exactly that – spending time with his family and relaxing on the beach after just a few hours of work.

The moral of this parable is often interpreted as a reflection on the value of simplicity and contentment in life. It encourages people to prioritise their well-being, relationships, and personal fulfilment over relentless pursuit of material success.

Keeping up with the Joneses (and the Diderots)

We've all heard about "Keeping up with the Joneses" in one form or another. If you haven't, it's the implicit pressure to keep up appearances and show off one's wealth. Actions become more externally motivated rather than internal. For example, if your neighbour starts renovating their house and building a swimming pool, even if you have no interest in swimming, you may feel pressured to renovate as well. This pressure also extends to more subtle areas, such as constantly buying the latest smartphone every year without any significant updates. Companies release new versions of their phones each year without real innovation because average people feel the need to keep up with the latest trends.

This social effect of keeping up with others also happens internally. It's called the *Diderot effect*, named after the French philosopher *Denis Diderot*. His story talks about how one scarlet gown ultimately plunged him into debt. Initially pleased with the gift, Diderot came to regret his new garment. Compared to his elegant dressing gown, his other possessions seemed tawdry and unsatisfying. He replaced his old straw chair with an expensive armchair covered in Moroccan leather; his old desk was replaced with a costly new writing table; his beloved prints were replaced with more expensive ones. "I was absolute master of my old dressing gown", Diderot writes, "but I have become a slave to my new one... Beware of the contamination of sudden wealth. The poor man may take his ease without thinking of appearances, but the rich man is always under a strain."

When combined together – Keeping up with the Joneses (external) and falling victim to the Diderot Effect (internal) – it becomes the fastest track into the rat race. The constant need to do what others are doing and buy things that don't add value to your life will lead to a life full of regrets. It's easy to become addicted to buying new things, but that feeling soon subsides and those things just become objects that own you while leaving you in debt.

Nobody looks back on their life and says, "I'm glad I bought that 55-inch TV when I was younger" or "Wow, that was a really good car I bought". It's the memories we make with friends and family, the challenges we overcome, the beautiful destinations we visit, and the time we spend with loved ones that truly matter. So why do we give our best years toiling away at work to buy material things that ultimately don't matter?

We see executives unable to spend time with their families because of work and justify it by saying they're working hard to provide for their family. But has the economy overinflated our idea of providing for our family? Is it now considered bad parenting if we can't purchase the latest gadgets for our kids?

What is Enough

There is nothing that can hinder true wealth more than not knowing when enough is enough. What is your definition of enough? Does having a roof over your family's head suffice? Is a yearly trip overseas enough? Is retiring early enough? Is a million dollars enough? Is there an arbitrary number? There is no right or wrong answer here. I do not advocate for a life of scarcity, but it's important to understand what truly brings satisfaction and joy to your life.

Being stuck in the rat race doesn't always mean having a 9-5 job. There's nothing wrong with having a fulfilling corporate job. Being stuck in the rat race means being forced to do something you hate in order to accumulate things you don't even like. For example, if you go skiing every year in Aspen with your whole family and spend $20,000 on your credit card, but you don't really enjoy skiing or the snow – you do it mostly for posting on social media – then you're trapped in a mindset that forces you to work just to pay those bills. However, if skiing and living in snowy mountains are truly your passion, you find ways to go to the snow regardless of the cost. Some people relocate to the mountains and find remote work or are content with having a simple job near the mountains rather than living in the city and spending thousands of dollars just to visit every year.

A book, a stranger, or even family members won't be able to tell you what your definition of enough is and what truly brings joy and value to your life. You must take the time to understand yourself and truly know what is enough.

Some folks know that if they don't have to work for the rest of their lives, that would be enough, while others are happy if they are able to provide for their family. If we can determine for ourselves what it means to have "made it," we will never be constantly chasing a moving goal post. We will be in a much better position to make big life changes or plan ahead for the things we want to do for the rest of our lives, rather than constantly being stuck in the rat race.

Action Point: Take some time to reflect on what motivates you – why do you do what you do? Consider these guiding questions:

• If nobody knew you were buying that thing, would you still buy it?

• If nobody knew you went to a particular place, would you still go there?

• What are the things that you do simply to keep up with others versus things you are genuinely passionate about?

Chapter Summary: Avoid the Rat Race by Knowing What is Enough

- The parable of the fisherman teaches the value of simplicity and contentment in life.
- "Keeping up with the Joneses" is the pressure to show off wealth and leads to external motivations.
- The Diderot effect describes how acquiring one new item can lead to a cycle of wanting more expensive possessions.
- Falling victim to both "Keeping up with the Joneses" and the Diderot effect leads to a life full of regrets and debt.
- True wealth comes from prioritising relationships, experiences, and personal fulfilment over material things.
- Understanding what truly brings satisfaction and joy to your life is important in defining "enough."
- Being stuck in the rat race means doing something you hate to accumulate things you don't even like.
- Reflect on your motivations and consider if you would still make certain choices even if no one knew about them.

Playing the Infinite Game

"Give me six hours to chop down a tree and I will spend the first four sharpening the axe." - Abraham Lincoln

Sharpen the Axe

Once upon a time, there was a young woodcutter named John. John had just started his career as a woodcutter and was eager to prove his worth. He had a big task ahead of him – to cut down an enormous tree in the forest. Excited and full of enthusiasm, John rushed to the forest with his axe in hand. Without wasting any time, he started swinging his axe at the base of the tree. However, after hours of relentless effort, he realised that his progress was negligible. The tree remained steadfast and unyielding. Frustrated and exhausted, John sat down to catch his breath. Just then, an old woodsman passing by noticed John's struggle and approached him.

"Son, why are you working so hard without taking a break?" asked the old woodsman.

"I need to cut down this tree as quickly as possible," replied John impatiently.

The old woodsman smiled gently and said, "Let me tell you a story. Once there were two woodcutters who were given the same task – to cut down one hundred trees each."

"The first woodcutter began immediately without any hesitation. He swung his axe repeatedly, working tirelessly throughout the day. On the other hand, the second woodcutter took some time before starting and spent most of it sharpening his axe."

John listened attentively as the old woodsman continued, "At the end of the day, when they counted their accomplishments, they were surprised to find that while the first woodcutter had cut down only six trees with his dull axe, the second woodcutter had successfully felled all ten trees with ease." The second woodcutter understood that taking some time to sharpen his axe would make his job easier and more efficient in the long run.

Reflecting on this parable, John realised that he had been too focused on rushing into action rather than preparing himself properly. He took the old woodsman's advice to heart and decided to take a break. He spent the time sharpening his axe meticulously, ensuring it was in its best condition. When John resumed his work, he found that with each swing of the now-sharp axe, the tree became easier to cut. His progress was faster, and soon enough, the massive tree came crashing down.

From that day forward, John understood the importance of sharpening his skills and tools before diving headfirst into any task. He learned that taking a moment to prepare and improve oneself would ultimately lead to greater success and efficiency in achieving his goals.

I had to start this section with a parable of sharpening the axe because it may sound obvious when we read about it, but when we are in the midst of a situation, we often fail to apply these principles. Our brains are not wired to see the faults in our decision making. In fact, our brains wouldn't have made those decisions if they thought they were wrong. Additionally, loss-aversion often prohibits us from making adjustments and further forces us into a deeper hole.

Short-Term Wins

I have a friend from college who took the same course as me. We were both aspiring software engineers back then. We took the same classes, hung out at the same places, and read mostly the same books. By the time we graduated, we both received offers from different companies. The first company (let's call it company A) was much smaller than the other one (let's call it company B). Company B was an international multifaceted company with thousands of employees and offered double the starting salary compared to company A.

My friend didn't hesitate and immediately chose company B without considering any other factors. He believed that working for such a prestigious company would guarantee prestige and success, and it did for a while. On the other hand, I thought about the long game. I knew that working for a smaller company like company A would give me a chance to make a bigger impact and learn more at this stage of my career. I knew it would force me to wear multiple hats in the company, doing various tasks for half the pay. I wanted to sharpen my axe first, I chose company A.

At first, it seemed like my friend had made the right choice. He constantly boasted about how much money he was making compared to all of us and how easy-going it was at work. Company B had thousands of other employees that there was no need for him to overexert himself, he was cruising day in day out. We soon realised that the projects we were working on were substantially different. I was working on projects with real-world impact, affecting thousands of users. My friend, on the other hand, was just doing internal company work that didn't have too much value.

Years had passed and I was steadily rising through the ranks at company A while my friend remained in the same position at company B. At the same time, the tone of our catch-ups was slowly shifting as he started feeling stuck in a dead-end job. During an economic downturn, his boss started to give him more work that he couldn't handle. He tried thinking about looking for a new job but he had become obsolete at that point. He had become complacent and lost his credibility due to maintaining legacy systems and doing the bare minimum for years on end. He had become a dull axe.

More than a decade have passed since then, and the lessons I've learned about playing the long game and investing in skill acquisition are still paying dividends for me. I have worked with multiple companies, constantly honing my skill with each move. I've traveled the world to solve their biggest problems and have risen through the ranks. My friend, however, has only changed one job and had one pay bump since then and has been stuck with company B unable to move. He had been blinded with the initial pay, not knowing it was a death sentence for his career.

This story is akin to sharpening the axe – it sounds obvious when we read about it in parables, but in real life, we are often blinded by short-term gains. Our brains tend to lean towards easy short-term rewards and instant gratification, instead of focusing on long-term compounding success.

Infinite Game

As a nomad entrepreneur, patience and having systems in place are crucial. It's easy to lose structure in your life when you no longer have to wake up early or worry about finances. That's why it's important to sharpen your axe before starting this journey and establish systems that will sustain your lifestyle, ensuring long-term success and stability.

One important aspect of playing the long game as a nomad entrepreneur is patience. It can be tempting to rush into action and try to achieve immediate results. However, taking the time to plan, prepare, and build a strong foundation will ultimately lead to greater success in the long run.

In addition to patience, having systems in place is crucial for maintaining structure and stability as a nomad entrepreneur. Without a routine or framework, it's easy to become disorganised and lose focus. By establishing systems for things like time management, financial planning, and goal setting, you can ensure that you stay on track and make progress towards your long-term objectives.

Just like how John learned the importance of sharpening his axe before cutting down the tree, as a nomad entrepreneur, it's essential to invest in skill acquisition and personal growth. Continuously improving your skills and knowledge will not only make you more valuable in the marketplace but also open up new opportunities for growth and advancement.

When my friend chose company B solely based on its higher starting salary, he failed to consider the long-term implications of his decision. While he initially enjoyed the financial benefits of working for a larger company, he soon found himself stuck in a dead-end job with limited prospects for growth. It was only a high paying job at the beginning, but as the years pass it was not able to keep up costs of living and inflation. Without growth, it had become a career ender.

On the other hand, by choosing company A and focusing on skill acquisition and making an impact early on in my career, I set myself up for long-term success. I was able to rise through the ranks, work on meaningful projects, and continuously increase my marketability. Even today, the skills I learned are still valuable as I made the shift from employee to entrepreneur.

The lesson here is clear – when making decisions about your career or any other aspect of your life, think beyond short-term gains. Consider how each choice will impact your long-term goals and aspirations. Invest in yourself by sharpening your skills, establishing systems for success, and being patient as you navigate this unique lifestyle.

Chapter Summary - Playing the Infinite Game

- Taking time to prepare and improve oneself leads to greater success
- Short-term gains can blind us from long-term success
- Investing in skill acquisition and personal growth is essential for long-term success
- Patience and having systems in place are crucial for a nomad entrepreneur
- Continuously improving skills and knowledge opens up new opportunities
- Consider long-term implications when making decisions as a nomad entrepreneur

Systems Thinking

"Strength does not come from physical capacity. It comes from an indomitable will." - Mahatma Gandhi

Limited Willpower

One little-known fact that everyone should be aware of is that we all have limited willpower. Each person has their own level of willpower, which can be influenced by factors such as upbringing and discipline. Despite these variations, it remains true that each of us only have a finite amount of willpower.

One of the most well-known studies on limited willpower is the "ego depletion" experiment conducted by *Roy Baumeister*. In this study, participants were asked to resist eating freshly baked cookies while completing a challenging cognitive task. The researchers found that participants who resisted the cookies performed worse on subsequent self-control tasks compared to those who did not have to exert self-control earlier.

Another study conducted by *Baba Shiv* and *Alexander Fedorikhin* examined the impact of decision-making on willpower. Participants were divided into two groups: one group was asked to memorise a two-digit number, while the other group had to memorise a seven-digit number. Afterward, they were given the choice between a slice of chocolate cake or a fruit salad as a reward. The study found that those who had to memorise the longer number were more likely to choose cake than those in the shorter number group, suggesting that making decisions depletes willpower.

Real-life examples that demonstrate limited willpower can be seen in various situations:

Dieting: Many people struggle with sticking to a diet plan throughout the day. They may successfully avoid unhealthy food choices in the morning but find it harder to resist cravings later in the day due to depleted willpower, resulting in late-night snacks and binging.

Procrastination: People often delay important tasks until later in the day or evening when they feel more fatigued. This can be attributed to limited willpower resources as they have already spent their self-control earlier in the day. This is why cramming is prevalent.

Impulse buying: Retailers strategically place tempting items near checkout counters, taking advantage of customers' depleted willpower after shopping for an extended period. Ever thought about why chocolate bars are placed near the checkout counter when you are about to pay and fruits/vegetables are always right by the entrance? The idea is that shoppers will give in to their impulses towards the end as their willpower depletes while they are walking around the store.

Addiction: Individuals struggling with addiction often find it challenging to resist cravings as their willpower diminishes over time. They may successfully avoid temptations for some time but become more vulnerable to relapse as their self-control weakens.

Eat The Frog

That's why there are several books, psychologists, and life coaches that advocate for "Eating The Frog" first, popularised by *Brian Tracy* in his book. This concept essentially advocates for doing the toughest thing that delivers the most value first thing in the morning while your battery is replenished from a full night's rest. This is exactly why some people wake up early in the morning to do their morning workout before going to work, prioritising their health and mental state even before the day begins.

Taking it one step further, from the book "Deep Work" by Cal Newport, the author researched how much quality work each individual can produce in any given day. He makes the point that in reality, we can only sustain up to four hours of high-quality work throughout the day. After those four hours, we are operating at a deficit. This is why when certain people pull all-nighters, they end up doing more unnecessary work because forcing yourself to work under this model introduces a lot of rework and errors. It's important to know that more hours does not mean more progress, busyness does not mean productivity.

If we consider both "Eating The Frog" and our capacity for deep work, we realise that there is only a limited amount of time during which our brains can produce high-quality work that could potentially bring value to the world. If you are an author, during this optimal state you can only write so many pages. If you are a software engineer, you can only code so much of an application. This is why sometimes we see ridiculously rich people wearing plain clothes all the time—they are reserving their willpower to make important decisions rather than wasting it on trivial things such as the colour of their shirt as each tiny decision depletes their willpower.

There is a popular concept attributed to *Peter Drucker*, a management consultant and author, that an average CEO's job is to make only a handful of critical decisions per day that have possible repercussions company-wide, rather than making many small decisions throughout the day that only affect a small number of people.

Powerful Habits

To enable you to sustain your willpower battery longer, there are two ways to create systems:

Making Sustainable Habits Easy: By designing your environment and routines in a way that encourages positive habits, you can conserve your willpower for more important tasks. For example, if you want to eat healthier, having pre-prepared meals or snacks readily available can make it easier to resist unhealthy options when your willpower is depleted.

Creating 'If Else' Decisions: By setting clear guidelines or rules for decision-making in advance, you can reduce the cognitive load of making choices throughout the day. For example, if you have a rule that you won't check social media until after completing your most important task for the day, you eliminate the need for constant decision-making about when to engage with distractions.

One of the key foundations of being an entrepreneur is creating products and services that people will find valuable. If you drain your willpower throughout the day on things that do not allow you to produce valuable work, it becomes much harder to sustain this lifestyle.

Chapter Summary: Systems Thinking

- Limited willpower is a fact that everyone should be aware of, as each person has their own level of willpower which can be influenced by various factors.
- Decision-making also deplete willpower, as shown by the study where participants who had to memorise a longer number were more likely to choose cake over a healthy option.
- Real-life examples of limited willpower include dieting, procrastination, impulse buying, and addiction.
- "Eating The Frog" advocates for doing the toughest task that delivers the most value first thing in the morning when willpower is replenished.
- According to "Deep Work," individuals can only sustain up to four hours of high-quality work per day before operating at a deficit.
- Reserving willpower for important decisions is important, as evidenced by rich people who prioritise decision-making over trivial matters.
- Creating sustainable habits and setting clear decision-making rules can help conserve willpower for more important tasks.
- Conserving willpower is crucial for sustaining a nomad entrepreneur lifestyle and producing valuable work.

Work-Life Balance Revisited

"Choose a job you love, and you will never have to work a day in your life." - Confucius

9-5 for 32 years

I've always loved work-life balance, but not in the traditional sense. The average career length is the typical 9am-5pm, Monday to Friday schedule for 32 years. This to me does not feel balanced to me. In fact, when you consider all the additional time it takes to get ready for work, commute, and think about work during your downtime, the actual amount of time dedicated to work is closer to 10-12 hours a day. If you take the whole weekend just recovering from work, that time becomes indirectly work-related too. This extra time surrounding the mandatory 8 hours of work is what they call Indentured Time – time that companies benefit from without compensating you. This can be from the daily commute, from the recovery time you use because of a stressful work day, from the time your boss calls you at wee hours of the night, from venting out with your partner about that incompetent coworker, or even when you're showering and inadvertently start contemplating about the problem at work. Unless you can completely shutdown work and compartmentalise it that it does not exist outside the office walls, indenture time often creeps up to you with you knowing it. The company benefits from this absolutely for free.

It gets worst as you progress in your career and climb up the ladder, the expectations only increase. You're expected to be available over weekends and stay later than 5pm. Everything seems designed to drain as much of your time as possible with as minimal value to you as possible.

If you haven't already realised it by now, let me tell you: time is infinitely more valuable than money. With ample time, anyone can earn any amount of money. Even the richest man on the planet has 24 hours a day and limited time on earth.

Redefining Balance

So, how do I define balance? It's about building a business that sets you up for life in just a few years. Sure, it may require working 10-12 hours a day for seven days a week during that period, but it's an investment in your future freedom. You are building your foundations and sharpening your axe. How does this sound for work-life balance: By dedicating yourself fully for a couple of years, you can avoid the need to work for the rest of your life.

We've seen people achieve this level of financial freedom before – why not you? Because what's the alternative? Working those same long hours for five days a week over 32 years?

The math speaks for itself.

- **Hours**: Approximately 10 hours a day (including all indentured time: preparation, commuting, etc)
- **Days**: 260 working days a year (roughly 5 days a week with some weekends due to being on call or higher up in the company)

- **Years**: Approximately 32 years (the average career length if you're constantly employable and healthy)

Working Hours x Working Days a Year x Years = Working Life

10 Hours x 260 Working Days x 32 Years = 83200 hours

Now, let's compare this to being an entrepreneur:

- **Hours**: 16 hours a day (assuming an extreme entrepreneur doing a startup)
- **Days**: 365 working days a year (let's exaggerate and assume no days off at the beginning!)
- **Years**: 3-5 years (this is where it gets interesting because most entrepreneurs won't last more than 5 years without their business gaining traction and earning money)

Working Hours x Working Days a Year x Years = Working Life

16 Hours x 365 Working Days x 5 Years = 29200 Hours

If you look at the potential returns and assuming more or less similar effort, it start to look as if being an employee is the riskier bet. To assume employment and good economies in the span of 32 years coupled with continuous good health and a long life after 65 start to sound like a tall order and puts your life on the hands of either luck or somebody else.

Let's be pessimistic for one moment and think "no, my business won't take off in 5 years", even if you double that, which is 10 years, that is 58400 hours. The book *Mastery* from "Robert Greene", teaches us that to master a craft takes 10,000 hours, and to be truly great hovers around 20,000 hours. From the greatest basketball players, to the world's greatest violinist, it took them approximately those hours to achieve what they do. From the book *Outliers* by *Malcolm Gladwell,* the author takes a look at everyone from rock stars to professional athletes, software billionaires to scientific geniuses. And the common denominator has always been time, they had significantly more time to hone their craft and do trial and errors to perfect it.

Are you then saying that you would rather spend 83200 hours of your life than to yourself? The truth is there is a price for certainty, the certainty of a paycheque every month coming in comes at a price of three decades of your life and if you're unlucky with economy, being unable to live the life you want at the end of it all. How many retirees do we hear that are living their best life during their twilight years? Does this sound like work-life balance to you?

Entrepreneurship is a craft, like any other trade, it needs time and mastery. You need to be willing to put in the hours, but the payoff is massively in your favour.

Retirement Money

As for the average amount of money in retirement as an entrepreneur, it's difficult to determine because there is no average. Depending on the business venture and its success, it could range from millions of dollars to a couple of hundred thousands, or maybe 0. However, what remains true is that for the fraction of time you invest compared to traditional employment, the returns have the potential to be astronomical. Let's consider $100,000 as a conservative estimate for the lowest amount. Why? Well, if your business has survived for more than five years, there's a good chance it's earning money. Otherwise, it would have closed down and you would either start another business or return to corporate work – going back to trading time for money.

If the maximum time required to build a potentially million-dollar business is just five years, then within an average career length of 32 years, you still have six opportunities to pursue such ventures, how do you then end up with zero dollars at retirement age if you continuously pursued entrepreneurship?

Of course, this is an oversimplification and all results vary. Everything has risks involved, and depending on your risk appetite it could also involve still keeping your day job as you pursue entrepreneurship. As an entrepreneur, you'll save time by avoiding the indentured time that traditional work requires. This means you can pursue multiple business ventures or other means of earning an income within a shorter period of time. So, if you take multiple shots at entrepreneurship in the first 3-5 years, the odds are in your favour. This is what wealthy people mean when they say "Make your own luck."

Think about how you envision work-life balance. Is it working for 32 years with only a small chance of significant rewards? Or is it dedicating yourself to extreme work ethic for five years and enjoying unlimited potential for rewards? What does balance mean to you? Personally, I love the idea of work-life balance that comes from building a successful business.

Chapter Summary: Work/Life Balance Revisited

- The traditional 9-5 schedule is not balanced due to additional indentured time you use just to prepare and recover for work.
- Balance is about building a business that sets you up for life in a few years.
- Working as an entrepreneur may require more hours and days initially, but it can lead to financial freedom in a shorter time frame.
- Comparing working hours, days, and years between being an employee and an entrepreneur shows that being an employee has a longer working life.
- Being an entrepreneur has the potential for higher returns compared to traditional employment.
- Retirement money as an entrepreneur varies but has the potential to be astronomical with less time invested.
- Pursuing multiple business ventures within a short period of time increases the odds of success as an entrepreneur.
- Work-life balance can be achieved by dedicating oneself to extreme work ethic for a few years and enjoying unlimited potential for rewards.

Keystone Reason

"Success is the sum of small efforts, repeated day in and day out." - Robert Collier

We all have a reserve in the back of our minds that helps preserve our self-esteem. This reserve is often veiled by one or more excuses. For example, you might say, "I could get fit if I just had time to workout," or "I can lose 10 pounds whenever I want, I just don't have the money to buy healthy food." These excuses serve as a shield for our self-esteem, protecting us from facing the truth.

In his book *Atomic Habits*, *James Clear* introduces the concept of a "Keystone Habit" – a habit that sets off a chain reaction of cascading effects. Let's take smoking as an example. When you smoke, the chemicals released by cigarettes affect your motivation to work out. Additionally, the damage done to your lungs makes exercising even more uncomfortable. As a result, it becomes easy to gain weight and feel sluggish, leading you to spend more time on the couch binge-watching TV shows. Smoking creates a negative feedback loop of habits that are hard to break.

On the other hand, identifying and cultivating positive keystone habits can have powerful and cascading effects on our lives. An example positive keystone habit is waking up early where we establish a routine that sets the tone for the rest of the day. By waking up early, we have more time to engage in self-care activities such as exercise, meditation, or reading, which can increase our energy levels and improve our overall well-being. This increased energy and sense of accomplishment then carries over into other areas of our lives, such as work or relationships, where we may find ourselves more focused, productive, and present. Furthermore, waking up early often leads to better time management skills and the ability to prioritise tasks effectively. All these positive effects essentially stem from just one positive key habit.

The Story We Tell Ourselves

Similarly, we all have what I like to call a *Keystone Reason* – a story we tell ourselves that can make all the difference in our lives. This reason can be either positive or negative. It's that one event, choice, or excuse that we believe has defined our lives and prevented us from achieving greatness.

We often look at others who have achieved what we desire and think they had it different. We believe they had some unfair advantage that gave them access to opportunities we could only dream of. We tell ourselves that if only we had been born into wealth or lived in a first-world country or won the lottery, things would be different for us. We cling to these external factors because they provide an excuse for why we haven't achieved our goals. They protect us from facing the reality that maybe we're just not good enough or haven't put in enough effort.

But the truth is, we need to confront this reality head-on. We must remove the veil of excuses and accept that we are the ones holding ourselves back. When our brains accept this cold hard truth, a shift occurs. Instead of focusing on external factors, our minds start to think about what is within our control. We ask ourselves, "If it's just me preventing me from achieving my goals, what can I do differently? What steps can I take to improve my situation?"

Successful people are able to identify and tackle their excuses head-on. They don't let external restraints define their lives. They start businesses with minimal capital, build online followings as faceless streamers, rise from ordinary citizens to ultimate stardom, and wake up at 4am as busy executives just to fit in a workout. They find ways to overcome the constraints they once believed were insurmountable.

I do not talk acceptance and taking action from being in an ivory tower. If you remember, I was born from a third-world country, I had to prove to immigration officer that I'm not a flight risk every time I just wanted to go on vacation. When I first moved abroad, companies subtracted the years of work I had already done when considering positions that I could be eligible for. To them, work I did in my home country did not count. I talk about acceptance and action from starting all the way to the bottom. We all have our advantages and disadvantages, that's just life, the question is always what are you going to do about it.

Acceptance = Freedom

Once we accept that we are the ones responsible for our lives – regardless of our circumstances – our brains go into overdrive. We begin searching for different paths and possibilities to achieve our wildest dreams. But it all starts with introspection; it begins with looking ourselves in the mirror and acknowledging that the constraint is within us. We may not be good enough yet, but there are things we can address and improve upon in order to reach our goals.

No one else can do this for us – not family members or friends. The responsibility lies solely with us. We must be willing to accept this reality and make the necessary shifts within ourselves.

Action Point: Take a moment to reflect on the story you keep telling yourself that is preventing you from pursuing your dreams. In a world of over 7 billion people, has no one achieved what you desire under similar circumstances? Consider that you may simply not have learned about them yet. Take the time to reflect and accept the external reasons you've been using as excuses, realising that they are just self-esteem preservation tactics

Chapter Summary: Keystone Reason

- We often make excuses to protect our self-esteem and avoid facing the truth.
- Identifying and cultivating positive keystone habits can have powerful cascading effects on our lives.
- Waking up early is an example of a positive keystone habit that can improve energy levels, well-being, time management skills, and productivity.
- We all have a Keystone Reason, a story we tell ourselves that can make a difference in our lives.
- We need to confront the reality that sometimes we are the ones holding ourselves back.
- Accepting responsibility for our lives leads to introspection and searching for different paths to achieve our dreams.
- The responsibility lies solely with us, and we must be willing to make necessary shifts within ourselves.
- Reflect on the story preventing you from pursuing your dreams and consider that others may have achieved similar goals under similar circumstances. Accept external reasons as excuses and realise they are self-esteem preservation tactics.

PART 2: FINANCE

Road To Riches

"The road to riches is not paved with gold, but with determination, hard work, and a relentless pursuit of your dreams." - Colin Powell

Same Effort, Uneven Rewards

My mentor once told me, "The effort it takes to do something for a $100 million market is the same effort it takes for a $1 million dollar market." At the time, his words didn't make sense to me, and I simply nodded in agreement. However, as I let his statement simmer in my mind and reflected on what he had actually said, it started to make more sense.

During my time working corporate jobs and moving from one company to another, I realised that the effort required of me was consistently the same, sometimes more, regardless of the size of the company. It didn't matter if I worked for a global corporation with headquarters in New York, London, and Australia or a small startup with only five employees. The toll it took on me mentally and physically was always more or less equal. The time it took to mentally prepare for work, the effort it took to get to and fro the office, and even the days needed to recover after long days of grinding. It all amounted to more or less the same.

I always gave 100% in everything I did, I noticed that no matter how hard I worked, the outcome remained unchanged. My paycheque might have been slightly higher when working for larger companies, but it wasn't enough to significantly change my life. I still had to deal with difficult clients and sometimes incompetent teammates. The hours remained, up to 10-11 hours including indentured time. It felt like nothing you did would be life changing, it was the epitome of being in a rat race.

Additionally, no matter how much I earned, the government would always tax me the same or even more if my income exceeded a certain threshold. It became clear to me that regardless of what job or industry I worked in — be it government agencies, universities, banking institutions, retail, logistics — everything was more or less the same. The pay increase was minimal, inflation would catch up eventually erasing any financial progress made. I felt constantly at the mercy of someone else's decisions and actions.

But then a thought occurred to me: If the effort required was always the same regardless —why can't it be my own business or endeavour? It would be the more or less the same effort but the rewards would be mine to reap. This realisation opened the floodgates of possibilities in my mind. I had been building software constantly for someone else, and see them reap the rewards from software I had built, why couldn't I do it for me? After all, it was my life on the line, and I didn't want to be a corporate slave forever.

The only difference was putting skin in the game, and doing it under my name.

How many of you out there are giving your all, only to receive the same pay over and over again? How many times have you covered for a co-worker, only for it to go unnoticed or unappreciated by management? Or worse, you are expected to pick up others' slack as part of your job?

The corporate job can be compared to a $1 million dollar market, the market is so small, that the biggest slice you can take won't be life-changing, it will only be barely enough to cover you through to retirement. In this market, if you're lucky and invest wisely while playing your cards right, you might earn $1 million dollars in 30-40 years, a millionaire by 65. This is where most people find themselves today—caught in the typical lifestyle of working a job, buying cars and fancy clothes, taking expensive vacations, but ultimately spending their lives paying off debt and mortgages.

Death Contract

Here's an interesting fact: The word "mortgage" comes from French law and means "death contract" or "death pledge." Interestingly enough, even the word "debt" sounds awfully close to "death" when pronounced.

It seems that many of us are content with staying in this $1 million dollar market—a market that is highly saturated and can only accommodate a limited number of people. We fail to fathom the existence of larger markets that are less saturated but still require more or less the same effort. We directly correlate effort with earning money. Therefore, when we think about a bigger market, we assume that it requires significantly more effort. And if we are already struggling within our current market, how could we possibly consider moving up a level? However, there are people out there who earn money while they sleep. They have built software applications, brands, or written books that continue generating income for them indefinitely. This is the secret, this is the $100 million market, exponential returns with more or less the same effort.

Simple Math

Let's look at some facts: The average person's career spans 32 years, from the time they graduate until retirement. On average, it takes 180 days to write a book and 90-120 days to build a simple software application. This is assuming you are doing it full time and have an idea of what you are doing, a complete novice would take more time. Now, imagine if you wrote a book that became a best-seller, earning money from royalties, book sales, and other means of distribution. In essence, you would have traded 180 days of work for 32 years of income. Even if you struggled with writing books and needed to write 10 books just to understand the industry and how it works, that would still only be five years—a mere 15% of the time needed for a typical 9-5 job. The difference in time is massive and the returns are asymmetrical. And that's just writing books. Nowadays, some individuals create one viral video on the internet and instantly become famous with millions of dollars at their fingertips. We need to challenge the notion that productivity and creating money are solely tied to hands on keyboards and butts in office chairs.

Code and Media

In his book *"The Almanack of Naval Ravikant,"* the author Naval explains that separating earning money from the time we have to physically work is key to scaling ourselves. As humans, we have limited hours in a day—eight for office workers or sixteen for chronic workaholics—but machines, scripts, products, code or media can work around the clock without rest. You only need to build once and potentially earn consistently, this won't happen on your first try, but I guarantee that the time to master this skill will most certainly be less than 32 years.

I can almost hear some readers saying, "I don't have the luxury of setting aside months to work on something that could potentially earn me money" or "I can't abandon my work and family for 180 days to write a book or build software or start a YouTube channel" or even "I don't have anything that can earn me passive income." To these individuals I ask: Can you not spend a few days or weeks each year working on yourself but you are willing to spend 32 years working for someone else?

I understand that life can get in the way and that working on something that can earn passive income requires planning and preparation. It's always easier said than done, as we all have our own unique circumstances. It would be unrealistic to expect anyone to drop everything and start immediately.

As you continue reading this book, I will discuss strategies to help you further prepare for this journey. However, there needs to be a shift in your mindset first—a belief that passive income is possible and that people are currently earning money while they sleep. You could be one of them if you plan properly and take action. Depending on where I am right now and where you purchased this book, I have already earned something from it. The time it took me to write this book was not 32 years; instead, I wrote it once and it separated how I earn my money from the time I physically did the work. This is called leverage—a concept well-known by entrepreneurs —and now you understand it too.

Chapter Summary: Road To Riches

- The effort required to work in a $1 million market or a $100 million market is the same.
- Effort required in corporate jobs is consistently the same regardless of company size.
- Pay increase in larger companies is minimal and taxes remain the same or even more.
- Realisation that own business or endeavour would require the same effort but rewards would be exponential.
- Many people are stuck in the $1 million market, living a typical lifestyle of debt and mortgages.
- The word "mortgage" means "death contract" and debt sounds similar to death when pronounced.
- People fail to consider larger markets that require similar effort and can generate passive income.
- Writing a book can trade 180 days of work for 32 years of income.
- Machines, scripts, products, code, or media can work around the clock without rest.
- Passive income requires planning and preparation but is possible with proper mindset and action.

Slow and Steady Index

"The harder I work, the luckier I get." - Thomas Jefferson

We Only Have the Present

First off, I want to say that I have nothing against Index Funds and the power of compounding. *Albert Einstein* did say compounding interest is the 8th wonder of the world. I believe it is a strong financial vehicle, my main issue is its speed. Have you ever heard of a 30-year-old who became a millionaire because of index funds? Mathematically speaking, there are only a couple of ways this is feasible:

1. Your parents were smart enough to invest in an index fund under your name when you were born. This means that the money has been compounding for 30 years and is now bearing fruit.

2. You started with a ridiculous amount of money to begin with. If you invested $500,000 by the age of 22, then by the time you're 30, you already have a legitimate money tree. However, procuring that initial $500k won't be from index funds.

That is the sad truth about these types of wealth-building vehicles — they only work if you had an unfair advantage to begin with. Otherwise, even if you started working at 22 and were financially savvy right off the bat, it would still take you 20-30 years to become a millionaire through this method. And that's assuming the economy stays strong and consistently yields good returns year after year.

In 2008, during the financial market crash, many people saw their life savings get wiped out by an external event they couldn't control. Imagine diligently saving year after year, only to be wiped out by decisions made by people on Wall Street when you're so close to retirement. It's like gambling for 30 years, hoping the economy stays strong and that inflation doesn't outrun your income rate. That is not something I am willing to bet on for my future.

Pristine Principal

Another unspoken rule about these types of retirement plans is that they require you to live on plain interest alone while leaving the principal untouched in order to sustain growth. This means that if you've saved up $1 million dollars and have a 5% interest rate per annum, you can live off the $50,000 per year without touching the principal amount. However, if you lower the value of the principal, your overall yearly income will be affected. For example, if you drop it to $500,000, then your 5% annual budget becomes $25,000. And when you factor in the inflation rate of the economy, which was estimated to be a 7-9% increase in 2023 due to the pandemic, you're essentially losing money every year just by the passing of time. And this is assuming you're already financially savvy. If you've buried your money in a bank account earning less than 1% interest, then you're already throwing money away.

Stress, The Silent Killer

Now let's assume the economy goes your way and inflation isn't as bad. Can you guarantee what will happen to your health after your career? At one point in my life, I was so obsessed with work that I neglected my health and had to face the consequences. I was bedridden for a couple of weeks due to the stress and lifestyle I had to endure in order to keep up with a top-paying job. This was an eye-opener for me. No amount of money was worth sacrificing my health for a few extra thousand dollars. I was fortunate enough to have realised this early on in my career and to have come back relatively healthy from that ordeal. While I'm not back to 100% compared to before I got sick, I'm in a much more stable state now.

But not everyone will be as lucky as me. We've all heard stories of people dropping dead at their workplace or developing terminal diseases due to workplaces that didn't care for their employees' well-being or simply due to excessive stress.

Stress is poison to us. When we are under distress, our bodies do not operate under normal circumstances. The normal bodily functions that enable us to recover day in and day out stop working properly. When we are constantly in fight-or-flight mode, we unknowingly deteriorate our physical, mental, and spiritual well-being. The worst part is that most of this deterioration is invisible to the naked eye. When we are under constant stress, we don't see our physical bodies changing, and there are rarely obvious signs of what is happening within our bodies. And when the signs do show up, it's almost always too late. Suddenly, you discover a small lump somewhere that could prove fatal.

Now imagine diligently saving year after year, counting every penny, and making sacrifices in hopes of a comfortable retirement, only to have your health pull the rug out from beneath your feet. This is no way to live. It's a lot of hoping and assuming things will go your way in the future. It's like throwing a pair of dice in the dark and betting your entire life savings on blind luck for favourable results. It's like testing the depth of waters with both feet or jumping headfirst into the unknown, hoping there are no rocks beneath the calm surface.

Rolling the Dice

The only way you can come out relatively unscathed from this ordeal is based purely on luck—luck that the economy, inflation, your health, and all other external factors work in your favour. And even then, with all the luck on your side, you may be forced to live a modest life without touching your principal amount out of fear that you won't have enough down the road. You won't even know how many years you have left.

How does this retirement plan work? Why do we believe it's the best way? What happens to the principal when we're gone? Does our family get it or does the government take it all? I'm not sure about you, but I don't want to wait until I'm in my 70s to find out. I want to live a full life while being able to provide for my family and live my best life. We all want to live our best lives in the present, not 30 to 40 years from now.

Chapter Summary: Slow and Steady Index

- Index funds and compounding interest are a strong financial vehicle, but they are slow in building wealth.
- Becoming a millionaire through index funds typically requires an unfair advantage through a large initial investment.
- The economy and external events can wipe out savings and investments.
- Retirement plans often require living off interest alone, leaving the principal untouched for growth, lowering the principal affects yearly income, especially when factoring in inflation.
- Saving diligently for retirement does not guarantee good health in old age given constant stress we are exposed to.
- Relying on luck for a comfortable retirement is not ideal, as it requires favourable external factors.
- A retirement plan based on luck may result in living modestly without touching the principal amount.

Create Value

"Given a ten percent chance of a 100 times payoff, you should take that bet every time. But you're still going to be wrong nine out of ten times." - Jeff Bezos

Half a Recipe

Again, I am not against compounding interest, many people consider it the 8th wonder of the world, and rightfully so. With basic mathematics and the passing of time, we can reap exponential rewards.

However, time in this wealth formula acts as a double-edged sword. We only start reaping the rewards towards the end of our lives. If we weren't lucky enough to be born into a wealthy or financially educated family, we begin our financial journey in our mid-twenties or even later. By then, it may feel too late. We could have been compounding our wealth for the past 20 years by simply existing, but that opportunity has passed. We must play with the cards we've been dealt.

So what's the real deal? You've read about compounding interest and it all adds up, but in the grand scheme of things, it still doesn't seem like the road to riches. Or perhaps it is a road to riches, but it's long and full of unexpected speed bumps that could derail your future dreams of retiring in the Caribbean.

If there's one idea you take away from this book, let it be this. The secret is that you're not seeing the whole picture. **Compounding interest is only half of the formula**. Yes, the wealthy use compounding to sustain and grow their wealth, but it's not what made them rich in the first place.

Unfair Advantages

Everyone has their own unique unfair advantage that they don't talk about, It feels like boasting about something others can't attain. It's like talking about how to grow taller when you were blessed with certain genes. In the previous chapter, I hinted at an unfair advantage - being born into a wealthy or financially smart family allows you to start compounding returns from day one. But don't lose hope; everyone has their own unfair advantage.

I didn't have any to begin with. I was born in a third-world country to an average family. My unfair advantage was being born with all my extremities and an appetite for learning. If you have these too, then you already have an unfair advantage. For someone like me, who had limited unfair advantage, here's the outline of my path:

1. Save as much as you can until you reach a point of decent returns.
2. Find a way to buy time by slowing down your burn rate.
3. Shift from a *Consumer mindset* to a *Producer mindset* and start creating things of value.

Save and Get Decent Returns

Everyone has their own definition of decent returns, so there's no one correct answer. It depends on your personal threshold for feeling financially secure. However, the general idea is that "decent returns" means having enough income to avoid constant worry about money. This could be earning 30% of your monthly income or just enough to pay the bills. It could even be zero if you're content with not earning any income for now.

This plan relies heavily on slowing down time or at least perceiving it that way. Time won't slow down if you're constantly worried about cash flow.

Here are my suggestions for saving as much as you can:

1. Cut unnecessary expenses: Take a hard look at your monthly expenses and identify areas where you can cut back. This can be tricky to determine, as there are things that are indirectly help you create value that may seem like an unnecessary expense, for example going to the gym helps you maintain a healthy mindset and keeps you healthy. What are the things that help you do what you do, but at the same time is not overly excessive. Does the $100 gym membership greatly increase your capability to create value compared to $30 one? If you are a physical therapist, probably. It all depends on your craft. This is something only you can answer and requires introspection of who you are and what you spend on.

2. Increase your income: Look for opportunities to increase your income, whether through a side hustle, freelance work, or asking for a raise at your current job. The more money you earn, the more you can save towards achieving financial freedom.

3. Prioritise debt repayment: If you have high-interest debts like credit card debt or student loans, make it a priority to pay them off as quickly as

possible. The interest charges on these debts can eat away at your savings, so getting rid of them will free up more money for saving and investing. The same way compounding works with investments, there is a concept called negative compounding. This is the reason loans and debt can set you back, as you could be paying for years and still only covering the interest. This is why student loans in America are so debilitating.

Again, the aim is first you save, so you can invest those savings and aim for decent returns for a bit. Decent returns is subjective depending on your risk threshold, but the returns just be able to sustain you so you can buy time.

Buy Time

Buying time is crucial on the journey to financial freedom. It allows you to focus on creating assets that generate passive income while minimising the need for active income from traditional jobs. In other words, how much time can you spend building yourself before having to rely on a 9-5 job to put food on the table. The truth is it's hard to focus on creating things of value when there are bills to pay and debt collectors knocking on your door. You are basically racing against the time it takes for you to become self-sufficient versus solely depending on a paycheque from an employer.

After buying yourself some time, there are several strategies you can employ to further extend that period by reducing your burn rate. Burn rate refers to the rate at which you spend money on both necessary and unnecessary expenses, causing your bills to pile up and forcing you back into work sooner than desired. Let's explore some effective ways to slow down your burn rate:

1. Minimise fixed expenses: one of the main expense is usually housing or accommodation, by picking a country that enables you to extend your buying power for a bit means more time for you.

2. Embrace minimalism: Adopting a minimalist lifestyle can help you reduce unnecessary spending and focus on what truly brings value and happiness into your life. By living with less, you'll be able to save more and have more time and freedom to pursue your passions.

3. Build an emergency fund: Having a financial safety net in the form of an emergency fund can provide security and give you the freedom to take calculated risks in pursuit of your financial goals. Also, it removes you from having to take on unnecessary debt with exuberant rates because of unexpected events, because life happens.

By slowing down your burn rate and focusing on building passive income streams, you'll be able to buy more time for yourself and create a sustainable path towards financial freedom.

From Consumer to Producer

Creating things of value is the key to accelerating your journey towards financial freedom. Instead of solely consuming and relying on others for your income, adopt a producer mindset and focus on creating your own opportunities. Here's how you can make this shift:

1. Identify your skills and passions: Take some time to reflect on what you're truly passionate about and what skills you possess. It could be writing, coding, speaking - anything. By identifying your strengths, you can leverage them to create valuable products or services that does not

require your time to earn income from. Always remember "build once, earn multiple times"

2. *Start multiple businesses*: Utilise your skills and passions to launch a variety of potential businesses. Consider selling handmade crafts online, providing consulting services within your area of expertise, or creating a blog or YouTube channel focused on your interests. Throw everything against the wall and see what sticks, this is exactly why you've bought time. While not every thing will work, this is your chance to see what will depending on your skills and passion.

3. *Embrace Digital Platforms that enable you to build at scale*: In today's digital age, there are countless platforms available that allow you to showcase and sell your creations. Though different platforms will come and go, the internet has made it easier than ever to share your talents with the world. Whether it's setting up an online store on platforms like Etsy or Shopify, self-publishing an e-book on Amazon Kindle Direct Publishing, or creating online courses on platforms like Udemy or Teachable - all the tools you need to build at scale are all there, you just need to make use of them.

By shifting from a consumer mindset to a producer mindset and actively creating things of value, you'll not only increase your income but also gain more control over your financial future.

Remember, financial freedom is not achieved overnight. It requires consistent effort and a strategic approach. By saving, buying time, and creating valuable assets that will potentially earn while you sleep, you'll be well on your way to achieving the abundance and freedom you desire.

Chapter Summary: Create Value

- Compounding interest is only half of the wealth formula
- Everyone has their own unique unfair advantage
- Save as much as you can until you reach a point of decent returns Find a way to buy time by slowing down your burn rate
- Cut unnecessary expenses and increase your income to save more
- Prioritise debt repayment to free up more money for saving and investing
- Buying time is crucial on the journey to financial freedom
- Minimise fixed expenses and embrace minimalism to slow down your burn rate
- Build an emergency fund to provide security and remove the need for unnecessary debt
- Shift from a consumer mindset to a producer mindset and start creating things of value

Exponential Gains

"Every artist was first an amateur." - Ralph Waldo Emerson

1000% Increase

This section could be placed in either the mindset or finance section, as it involves a shift in how we view earning money. Let's consider a simple thought experiment: when was the last time you heard of someone receiving a 1000% increase in pay overnight? Think about the best-performing employee you know, someone who goes above and beyond for their company. Have you ever heard of them getting promoted two levels above their current position or receiving double their salary?

In my decade of working for various companies, I've never seen or heard of such an extreme reward for exceptional performance. Instead, it is more common for a company to gift you a watch after decades of service—it's an underwhelming gesture that seems to say, "Thanks for your time, now get out."

However, for individuals who create valuable products and services, experiencing a significant jump in income is not uncommon. Take, for example, a band that has been performing for years but suddenly gets discovered and starts selling out Madison Square Garden. Or consider the ride-sharing application that disrupted the taxi industry or the streaming service that made traditional television programming obsolete. There are also authors who faced rejection from numerous publishers before finding success with one book that launched them into stardom. And let's not forget about introverted gamers who publish their games online and amass millions of subscribers. There are even doctors turned coders turned YouTube sensations. There are podcasters who interview prominent figures. These ordinary individuals shifted their mindset to that of a creator and went from earning an average income to making millions seemingly overnight.

But we know better, these success stories didn't happen overnight—they were building behind the scenes long before they achieved widespread recognition. Nonetheless, it's clear that on the entrepreneurial or creator path, an exponential jump from zero to a million-dollar income is more reality than fiction—and these are just the stories we know. If you dig deeper, you'll find software engineers quietly building their own products and services online, generating thousands of dollars without anyone even knowing. You'll see people from various industries creating a similar products or offerings that disconnect their time from income and essentially building once and earning multiple times.

Law of Effection

In the book *Millionaire Fastlane* by *MJ DeMarco,* he talks about the *Law of Effection* (sic), simply put if you can reach or impact a millions of people, directly or indirectly, you will inevitably earn millions regardless of what you do. If you are a professional baseball player and entertain millions of people you become a millionaire. If you are a Surgeon that operate on big Hollywood stars, you indirectly reach millions of people, you become a millionaire. Even those behind the lime light the Laws of Effection (sic) still applies. If you own a garbage collection company, that collects rubbish all over the country indirectly affecting millions of people by the service you provide, you become a millionaire. On the other hand, if you were the garbage collector working for the owner, directly collecting garbage couple of houses a day, and only a few hundreds of the span of your career, you will never be a millionaire, and earn exponential gains. (Unless of course, you have the power of compounding but that's beside the point)

Booms Everywhere

During the AI boom, similar to the dot com boom, many engineers capitalised on creating offerings that met a pressing need. In the early days of the dot com boom, engineers developed products and services that transformed businesses, allowing them to operate at a 10x level or reach a 10x audience. For instance, *MJ De Marco,* the author of *"Millionaire Fastlane,"* created a website for booking limousine services online—an innovation that wasn't common at the time. By pioneering such a service,

De Marco significantly increased his net worth. Today, numerous engineers are leveraging AI to build previously unimaginable services with ease. These individuals don't need fame to earn millions of dollars or live a life of early retirement. They blend in with ordinary people at neighbourhood cafes—unaware that they are worth millions—simply living their lives without worrying about their next paycheque.

There was also an NFT boom recently where several artists created value by recognising its potential. The quick-thinking creators who developed scripts generating multiple NFTs experienced an incredible surge in income within a short period of time. Earning enough to not have to worry about getting a day job for the rest of their lives, an exponential 1000% jump. Regardless of one's stance on NFTs or their current real value, it's undeniable that these artists earned 1000% more than what they were previously making.

In Part 3, I will discuss the core competencies necessary for adopting a creator mindset and becoming a digital nomad. But for now, let's focus on shifting our mindset regarding how money is earned.

Linear Vs Exponential Returns

As former employees, we've been conditioned to view wealth creation as a linear process—slowly climbing up the ranks while being content with annual increases of 4-8%, the most extreme would be 20% increase if you change jobs. This mindset has been reinforced by banks, investment vehicles, and corporations that employ us. Our index funds may earn us 8-10% annually if we're lucky, and job promotions rarely result in a significant spike from our current salary.

In my experience working for various companies across different industries, I noticed that during interviews, prospective employers would always ask about my previous salary and anchor their offer on that rather than the perceived value I could bring to their company. It didn't matter if I had the solution to their biggest problem or solved million dollar problems; if my previous income was $50,000, they would offer me $65,000-$75,000 and expect me to be thrilled with the increase. After encountering this countless times, I started inflating my previous salary to see if it would lead to higher offers. It did. However, there was an upper limit—I couldn't claim that I earned $1 million at my previous job as a software engineer and expect a $1.2 million offer at the next one. It simply didn't work that way.

Consumer to Producer

The hard limit imposed by traditional employment and witnessing the potential for exponential returns ultimately pushed me to transition from an employee mindset to an entrepreneur mindset. As an employee, no matter how many hours I worked or how much effort I put in, my bottom line remained unaffected—aside from receiving shallow praise and a pat on the back from my employers. This contrasted with what could be achieved through the same level of effort as a creator or entrepreneur: exponential gains in the future. I had previously worked with large corporations and developed e-commerce sites and stock trading platforms—yet at the end of the day, it was the companies profiting from these applications while I was limited by an annual salary imposed upon me. If only I had built those platforms for myself, I could have continued reaping rewards long after completing the initial work. Again, build once, earn multiple times.

Transitioning to a creator mindset is not easy for most people. The idea of experiencing exponential gains in a short amount of time may sound like something out of a storybook—but if you actually were to write *that* storybook, you would realise it's more reality than fiction.

The most challenging aspect is the perceived reality—creators and entrepreneurs may have close to zero income for years on end. This is the nature of the beast, and during this period of building, friends, family, and society may pass judgment and question your life choices. Doubt creeps in constantly. Just ask the aspiring actress working odd jobs as a bartender to make ends meet or the startup founder who's not paying themselves because they believe in their business.

This relentless judgment can be soul-crushing. It's at this point that many people give up and retreat to the safety of a monthly paycheque. To withstand the storm, continue growing, and maintain a positive outlook is a challenge that not everyone is prepared to face. Those who have overcome these obstacles and gone on to become millionaires know this well. We've heard their stories—they talk about how no one believed in them, but they persevered even when they felt like giving up.

When success finally arrives, it feels like floodgates have opened—but until then, it may seem like nothing is happening for months on end. The trick is to remain patient while the seeds you plant take time to grow. After all, you don't constantly dig up a seed after planting it and demand an instant tree—do you? As *Naval Ravikant*—an angel investor in Silicon Valley—said: "Be impatient with action and patient with the result." So ask yourself: Are you willing to face these challenges head-on? Or would you rather spend 20 years at work and potentially receiving a silver watch with a company logo engraved on it?

Chapter Summary: Exponential Gains

- Employees never receive a 1000% increase in pay overnight, even for exceptional performance.
- Individuals who create valuable products and services can experience a significant jump in income.
- The *Law of Effection* states that if you can reach or impact millions of people, you will inevitably earn millions.
- Wealth creation is often viewed as a linear process with slow growth and small annual increases.
- Transitioning from a consumer to a producer mindset can lead to exponential gains in the future.
- Transitioning to a creator mindset is challenging and may involve years of close to zero income and judgment from others.
- Perseverance is key for those who have become millionaires—they faced doubt and overcame obstacles.
- Success may take time and patience, but the rewards can be worth it compared to years spent working for someone else.

Till Debt Do Us Part

"Wealth is not about having a lot of money; it's about having a lot of options." - Chris Rock

Negative Compounding Effect

Debt is a topic that I wanted to touch on as well. It is a double-edged sword that can cut both ways, and your perception of debt can easily derail your plans depending on how well you use it. One of the overarching themes of this book is compounding, which plays a role in what you create, your mindset, the skills you master, and how you handle your finances.

When you realise the true power of compounding in everything you do, not just in finances, you start unlocking rewards that you never dreamed of.

Negative compounding, on the other hand, is a potential pitfall that everyone should steer clear of. Have you heard of the *Broken Windows Theory*? Essentially, it's observed that when a building in an ordinary neighbourhood has a broken window that isn't addressed promptly, it starts to invite more broken windows. Juveniles begin breaking more windows and vandalising the area because they perceive that the building isn't cared for and no one is watching. Leave a car with a broken window overnight in a public place, and by morning there's a chance all the windows will be broken and the tires will be sitting on cement blocks. The broken window phenomenon demonstrates the negative compounding effect of not addressing something early on. A small issue can quickly escalate into something unmanageable if left unattended.

Debt is a catalyst for negative compounding effects. If you take on debt to pay bills because you can't afford them, you could easily find yourself in even more debt. Debt interest adds to the original amount borrowed, creating a cycle where it becomes increasingly difficult to pay off what's owed. For example, if your original debt was $100 with an interest rate of 10%, you would have to pay $110. If you couldn't afford to pay that off the next month, the interest would compound on top of $110 instead of $100. With each tick of interest accruing, it becomes easier to fall into a cycle of taking on more debt to pay for previous debt.

I discuss debt because it's important to have your finances sorted out on your journey to becoming a digital nomad entrepreneur. Don't take on debt just to take a gamble. Ideally, you should have your finances in order so that you can stay productive while on your journey. The nomad lifestyle is already stressful and requires significant changes and adjustments. The last thing you want is to constantly worry about debt following you around, making time your enemy. The rich make time their friend because only with time can the products and services they create grow.

Double-Edge Sword

What makes debt tricky is that it can also be used for good. If used correctly, it can be a vehicle that accelerates your path. If you take on debt and use it to help you achieve your goals faster, and you're able to pay it off quickly, then it's not much of a problem. Some might argue that they take on debt because they can't afford their goals, but that's not necessarily true. Let's say you have $100,000 in life savings, and your business requires $100,000 as well. Instead of putting all your savings into it all at once, you could take on half the amount in debt and use half of your savings. This way, if there is an emergency expense like a broken tire or hospital bills, you won't be left with zero money and forced to incur more debt. This strategy gives you some wiggle room for unforeseen circumstances.

This isn't an instruction manual for you to follow blindly but rather an example to prove a point, and could be an oversimplification of how to manage debt. Each person has their own circumstances and risk tolerance. It's important to assess your individual situation and act accordingly. Remember to always address events that negatively compound as soon as possible, no matter what advantages or disadvantages life has thrown at you.

Chapter Summary: Till Debt Do Us Part

- Debt can have both positive and negative compounding effects
- Negative compounding effect occurs when small issues are left unattended and escalate into bigger problems
- Debt can lead to a cycle of taking on more debt to pay off previous debt, making it difficult to break free from the cycle
- It is important to have your finances sorted out as a digital nomad entrepreneur to avoid constantly worrying about debt
- Debt can be used for good if used correctly and paid off quickly
- Taking on some debt while using savings can provide a safety net for unforeseen circumstances
- Managing debt should be based on individual circumstances and risk tolerance levels
- Address events that negatively compound as soon as possible, regardless of life's advantages or disadvantages

Taxes

"Taxes are the price we pay for a civilised society." - Oliver Wendell Holmes Jr.

Two Things that will remain constant

They say there will always be two things that remain constant: taxes and change. Another saying goes, "Tax is the subscription you pay to live in a country." We cannot talk about being a nomad without addressing the subject of taxes. While online resources often discuss accommodation, food, and visas when it comes to becoming a digital nomad, tax is a concrete aspect that must be dealt with. The last thing you want is a government agency behind you because you neglected to sort out your taxes. Numerous businessmen, celebrities, and politicians have faced consequences simply because they failed to take the time to handle their taxes. This may not be the most alluring subject, but it is integral nonetheless. So let's rip off the band-aid and get on with it.

Now, the constraint of this book is that I cannot discuss every possible tax law in each country; otherwise, this would turn into an accounting book. However, I can provide guideposts that can act as starting points for you to check and be aware of before making the leap. Also, it is important to note that this book does not act as a financial advisor or serve as your go-to resource for paying taxes or sorting out your finances. The lessons here provide guidance on key considerations for being a digital nomad. It's important to consult with your local accountant or refer to local tax laws for a proper breakdown of what you need to know based on your individual circumstances.

Tax Residency

Tax residency usually refers to where your business resides and where you are legally required to pay taxes based on your income. This can vary from country to country in terms of what they consider taxable income. For example, some countries may require you to pay taxes even if you are not residing within their borders, while others may exempt you from paying taxes based on the number of months you reside in their country.

There are two main things you need to consider: your tax residency as an individual and where you are currently earning income. For instance, if you are based in Australia, living in Thailand, and your business solely operates in the United States, where do you pay income tax? Some countries impose taxes on each product sold, while others tax annual income with deductions or exemptions.

For instance, certain countries do not require you to pay income tax or require only a fixed amount regardless of your income. The rich take advantage of this. Simple math shows us how much potential earnings you can retain with tax residency. If you earn $1 million annually but your business is based in a country that imposes a 40% tax rate, your take-home pay is only $600,000. In a country with a fixed tax rate that requires only $50,000 to be paid, you would have kept $950,000 for yourself and your family. That's $350,000 more for the same amount of work simply because of being based in a different country.

300k Salary versus Business Profit

When you become an entrepreneur, you have more options to structure your business in a way that maximises your earnings within the legal system. This is because entrepreneurs take all the risks of starting a business and provide employment opportunities, ultimately contributing to the government and economy. Thus, they also reap the rewards. If government agencies were stricter on taxing entrepreneurs, it would discourage people from starting their own businesses and potentially hindering economic growth. It would be a lose-lose situation for both sides. Asymmetrical rewards are necessary to entice people to take risks, this is the secret why the rich get away with paying less tax.

Some people may argue that it's unfair for the rich to be taxed less when individuals working 9-5 jobs are taxed 30-50% of their income. The discrepancy is mind-blowing if we look at the math. If an executive earns $300,000 and gets taxed at 50%, they are essentially taking home only $150,000. However, if a properly structured business earns the same amount, they can take home twice as much because they may not have to pay as much in taxes. While I am aware that taxes do not work exactly this way and are charged progressively, I have oversimplified it to make a point and avoid delving too deep into the technicalities of taxes in this book.

The sad reality is that the effort and stress required to be a top executive earning that much is similar to running your own business. Similar to the effort it takes to work for a million dollar market is the same effort for a hundred million dollar market. However, businesses have more at stake day in and day out. Executives can get fired but still find other jobs, whereas if businesses go bankrupt, it can wipe them out. The rewards are always asymmetrical because of the risks incurred.

A top executive may receive a bonus of $300,000-$1,000,000 by sacrificing time with their family and practically living in the office. On the other hand, a business can earn anywhere from $0 to $10,000,000 depending on its market and reach. It could take 30 years to become a top executive with such earnings. Plus, you don't achieve that by going home early Monday through Friday either; you achieve it by arriving early and leaving the office late. Meanwhile, a business or product you create can have unlimited earning potential in a much shorter amount of time by having more leverage. We've heard numerous stories of seemingly ordinary individuals writing books that earn millions or content creators becoming trending sensations and never needing to work again. We've seen engineers take advantage of dot com/AI booms setting themselves up for the rest of their lives. Entrepreneurs disrupt existing norms and become the new standard with people relying more on their products.

Opting for a $300k salary in corporate work may seem like the safe bet, but it takes its toll on you in terms of time and taxes. The rich understand this and adjust their strategies to reap better rewards in less time while minimising their tax obligations.

Chapter Summary: Taxes

- Taxes are a constant aspect of being a nomad and must be dealt with
- The book provides guideposts for understanding taxes as a digital nomad, but consult with a local accountant for specific details
- Tax residency refers to where you are legally required to pay taxes based on your income and can vary from country to country
- Consider both your individual tax residency and where you are earning income from when determining tax obligations
- Different countries have different tax laws, some may exempt you from paying taxes or require only a fixed amount regardless of income
- Being based in a different country with lower taxes can result in significantly higher take-home pay
- Entrepreneurs have more options to structure their businesses to maximise earnings within the legal system
- Properly structured businesses will pay less in taxes compared to individuals earning the same amount as employees
- The effort and stress required for top executives is similar to running a business, but the rewards are asymmetrical
- Businesses have unlimited earning potential in a shorter amount of time compared to traditional employment
- Entrepreneurs understand how to adjust strategies to minimise tax obligations while maximising rewards in less time.

Time is the Ultimate Luxury

"The two most powerful warriors are patience and time." - Leo Tolstoy

Time Frugality

The poor is frugal with money, the rich is frugal with their time.

The poor are often frugal with their money, always looking for ways to save a few dollars here and there. But the rich understand that their time is their most valuable asset, and they are frugal with it.

I once had a friend who would always choose the longer route on road trips to avoid tolls. Let's say the toll was $20. So, instead of paying the toll and saving time, we would spend an extra 30 minutes taking the longer route. In total, we wasted 2 hours of our combined time just to save $20. We could have used that time to do things we actually enjoyed - take a leisurely walk on the beach, savour a long dinner, or watch a movie together. But instead, we were stuck in traffic trying to save a few bucks.

The rich understand the value of their time. If they know that their time is worth $1000 per hour, they wouldn't hesitate to pay a $20 toll to save themselves from wasting precious hours in traffic. They know that their time can be better spent on high-quality activities that bring them joy and fulfilment. Or they could've spend that creating things of value. They could've used that time sharpening their minds in order to increase their self perceived hourly rate, and in turn their net worth.

Cutting costs is a race to the bottom, you can only save so much dimes and pennies to try to move the needle. Increasing your reach and value has potentially unlimited returns. Have you ever heard of an earnings cap from the rich? Where a person can only earn a maximum specified amount of dollars? There is no such thing. There is a limit to the bottom though, a soft limit of $0 and a hard limit when bank stop giving you credit to incur more debt.

Only time gives you leverage to increase your value.

Trains and Planes

Consider airplanes and trains. Even if *hypothetically* if both modes of transportation cost the same amount of money to build, by putting more bells and whistles to the train to elevate its costs, planes are still exponentially valuable than trains, because of the speed it can get you from one place to another. The rich understand that every minute wasted on a slower mode of transportation is equivalent to throwing away money. If someone earns $10,000 an hour, sitting on a slow train means they are essentially throwing away that amount of money. This is the reason why there is no such thing as private trains, only private jets.

The same principle applies to express lanes in queues. I once heard a story about a wealthy man who was going to a fancy restaurant with his father. His father couldn't understand why they couldn't just wait in line like everyone else, he didn't know his son was rich yet. The wealthy man explained that every minute they spent waiting in line was costing them money - money that he could have earned to cover the costs of the meal in the restaurant and more. That man was *Alex Hormozi, an entrepreneur running $100 million businesses.*

The rich simply do not waste time. They understand the value of every minute and how it can be better spent on activities that bring them true fulfilment and success.

Which Came First?

One could argue that the reason the wealthy can afford to bypass time constraints, and essentially not wait in line, is because they are already rich. They can pay to not wait in line. However, this is a false causation and correlation. The truth is, they became rich because they were smart with their time. While others wasted their lives on low-value activities, the wealthy made the most of their time by creating value. Wealth then became a natural byproduct of their efforts.

To illustrate this point, let's consider someone who spends their day waiting in queues for the latest phone, taking longer routes to avoid tollgates, and watching television all day. Is that person really likely to be wealthy? It's unlikely. Although that is an oversimplification, we cannot simply comprehend someone who waste their whole day to become someone of high-value. Simply put, how do you increase intrinsic value by wasting time? Then why do we reverse causation when someone who ensures their time is spent on quality activities inevitably becomes wealthy?

This concept is often misunderstood. The reality is that everyone has the potential to become rich with enough time. Even if we had just $1.00 at 1% interest per annum, we could become billionaires with a measly 231,742 years of compounding. Wow, if only I was a vampire. The constraint each one of us faces is time - we all have a finite amount of it on this earth. No matter how much wealth we accumulate, we can never buy more time.

Would you Accept 10 Million Dollars?

There was viral video where a younger man was asked if he would be happy with $10 million dollars. "Of course," he replied, making a face that implied the question was dumb. The older man then asked, "What if I told you that once you accept the money, you would only have 24 hours left to live, Would you still be happy?" The reaction on the younger man's face showed it all, he had been made a fool and the point was made - money is often assumed to be the most valuable thing, but in reality, time is the ultimate luxury.

Wealth Has Seasons

Wealth and time come in different flavours depending on our age and stage of life. Wealth accumulated in your 70s looks completely different from wealth accumulated in your 20s or 30s. When you're young, wealth affords you luxuries and experiences that may not be as appealing when you're elderly. Our dreams and aspirations also change with age - a person in their 50s may dream of retiring and supporting their grandkids while traveling the world, while someone in their 30s has different priorities. Regardless of what our dreams look like, we have a small window of opportunity to make them come true.

We should all strive to be smart with our time like the wealthy individuals who understand its true value. By prioritising efficiency and productivity, we can make the most of our limited time on this earth and create wealth as a byproduct of our efforts.

Managing Time

Time frugality is a concept that the rich understand and prioritise. They realise that time is their most valuable asset and they are willing to invest in it wisely. While the poor may focus on saving money in small ways, the rich understand that their time is worth far more than any amount of money.

This mindset is evident in various aspects of life. Whether it's choosing the most efficient mode of transportation or avoiding long queues, the rich are willing to pay for convenience and save themselves precious time. They recognise that every minute wasted on low-value activities is equivalent to throwing away money. This is why the poor has no issues with doom scrolling social media for hours on end.

It's important to note that wealth and time go hand in hand. The wealthy didn't become rich by chance or luck; they became wealthy because they were smart with their time and in turn have more time to create luck. While others wasted their lives on unproductive activities, the wealthy focused on creating value and making the most of their time.

In the end, money may be seen as valuable, but time is truly the ultimate luxury. By prioritising efficiency, productivity, and smart use of our time, we can create wealth as a natural byproduct of our efforts. Let us learn from the mindset of the wealthy individuals who understand the true value of time and make every moment count towards our success and fulfilment.

Chapter Summary: Time is the Ultimate Luxury

- The rich understand that their time is their most valuable asset and are frugal with it.
- Cutting costs is limited in its impact, while increasing value has unlimited returns.
- Wealth and time are interlinked, and the wealthy became rich by being smart with their time.
- Time spent waiting or on low-value activities is equivalent to throwing away money for the rich.
- Money is often assumed to be valuable, but in reality, time is the ultimate luxury.
- Wealth and time have different meanings and priorities at different stages of life.
- Everyone has a finite amount of time on Earth, regardless of wealth accumulation.
- By prioritising efficiency and productivity like the wealthy, we can create wealth as a byproduct of our efforts.

PART 3:
COMPETENCIES

Attract Attention

"The attention you give to anything is the most precious gift you can give." -
Richard Carlson

Did You See the Gorilla?

Have you ever wondered why we say 'pay' attention instead of 'give' attention or 'share' attention? It's because paying attention takes a toll on us. It depletes a finite resource. We are limited in how much attention we can give.

In a social experiment, people were asked to count the number of times a ball was passed around by a group of people in a short video. At the end of the video, they were asked if they noticed a gorilla passing by. Shockingly, many people did not see the gorilla even though it was clearly visible. The gorilla lingered for several seconds before leaving the frame. In any normal scenario, you would have noticed and reacted to a gorilla suddenly appearing.

This experiment shows that we often underestimate the value of attention as a resource. We think big corporations are only after our money, but they also want our attention. They are willing to pay millions, if not billions, of dollars just to get it. That's why social media platforms offer free access to their applications. They don't earn from your pictures or comments; they earn from your attention. Once they have your attention, they can subtly slip in advertisements that you may not even notice.

How the Brain Works

To understand why companies are willing to pay so much for our attention, we need to delve into how our brain works. In book *Thinking Fast & Slow* by *Daniel Kahnemann*, he explains that our brain operates in two main processes: the deliberate and effortful mind (prefrontal cortex) and intuitive and automatic mind (amygdala). The deliberate mind is what we hear when we think to ourselves - it's like internal dialogue. The automatic mind runs in the background and does most of the heavy lifting in our day-to-day lives.

For example, when we accidentally touch a burning stove, we don't pause, take time, and think about removing our hand. The signal from the heat goes straight to our brain, and our brain instantly reacts by pulling our hand away. Understanding how our brain operates is crucial in realising why our attention is such a valuable resource.

Subliminal Messaging

When we mindlessly scroll through social media feeds, we become deeply invested and seek dopamine hits from visual stimulation. We don't foresee the long-term implications of advertisements that randomly appear. Suppose you're scrolling through beach photos, and suddenly an advertisement for a luxury car appears. You may not pay attention to it at the time, but it plants thoughts in your mind. When you eventually go to the beach months later, you might have a random desire to buy a luxury car, without realising where this desire came from.

This process doesn't happen overnight with just one advertisement. It's a gradual accumulation and familiarity of multiple subliminal messages that shape our desires over time. Companies spend billions of dollars and employ thousands of psychologists to scatter advertisements throughout our daily lives, all in pursuit of capturing our attention.

This is why video streaming platforms are investing heavily in content creators today. Instead of relying on marketing professionals to figure out what society is paying attention to, they hire content creators who have organically built communities around them. These creators share their everyday lives and build connections with their audiences. Companies can then strategically place advertisements within this content, targeting specific niches.

Let's do some simple math to understand this point further: if a content creator garners ten million views each month, a company can pay for a short ad on their video and instantly reach those ten million viewers. That audience could consist of single moms or young gamers, depending on the content created by the creator. It is highly targeted and has a higher chance of conversion rates for a specific company. Compare this to paying for a billboard in Times Square - even if it reaches ten million pedestrians, they may not be your target market. A percentage of random people walking in Times Square may not even understand English. By working with content creators who have highly engaged audiences within specific niches, companies can achieve reach the right consumers resulting in more sales.

The shift in marketing has moved away from traditional methods like billboards towards leveraging existing audiences through content creators.

Great Power, Great Responsibilities

As nomad entrepreneurs, we need to reconsider what competencies are essential for running a successful business. It's not just about traditional skills like balancing accounts or finding suppliers. We must adapt to the evolving economy and understand the power of attention, both in terms of capturing it for our own business and being mindful of how it is being captured by others.

In today's digital age, attention is a currency. It's what drives engagement, influences decisions, and ultimately determines the success or failure of a business. Just like money or time, attention is a limited resource that we must use wisely.

As entrepreneurs, we have the power to capture and hold the attention of our target audience. Whether it's through compelling content, innovative products, or exceptional customer service, we can create experiences that not only capture attention but also keep it.

With this great power comes great responsibility. We must be mindful of how we capture and utilise attention. We should strive to provide value rather than simply seeking to exploit it for short-term gains. By building trust and fostering meaningful connections with our audience, we can create long-lasting relationships that go beyond fleeting moments of attention. At the same time, we must be aware of how others are capturing our attention. In a world filled with distractions and constant stimuli, it's easy to fall prey to subliminal messaging and manipulation. We need to stay vigilant and discerning, making conscious choices about where we direct our attention.

So how do we strike this balance? How do we capture and hold attention while staying true to our values and maintaining ethical practices?

The answer lies in authenticity. Authenticity builds trust and credibility. When we are genuine in our intentions and transparent in our actions, people are more likely to give us their attention willingly. By delivering value consistently and aligning ourselves with causes that matter to our audience, we can create a mutually beneficial relationship based on trust.

Practice the art of attracting attention and be mindful of what you pay attention to.

Chapter Summary: Attract Attention

- Paying attention depletes a finite resource and we often underestimate its value
- Companies are willing to pay for our attention and use subtle advertisements to shape our desires
- Mindlessly scrolling through social media feeds allows for subliminal messaging to influence our desires
- Video streaming platforms are investing in content creators to strategically place advertisements within their content
- Attention is a currency in today's digital age and determines the success or failure of a business
- Entrepreneurs have the power to capture and hold attention through compelling content, innovative products, and exceptional customer service
- Striking a balance between capturing attention and maintaining ethical practices lies in authenticity

Build Leverage

"Give me a lever long enough and a fulcrum on which to place it, and I shall move the world." - Archimedes

What is leverage? Before writing this book, I had the privilege of working with a Senior Partner in a prestigious firm who acted as my mentor. He constantly emphasised the importance of leverage in order to reach the next level. However, when I asked him to explain what exactly that meant for someone in my position, he struggled to put it into words. To him, it seemed like something I should already know based on my unique circumstances and skills. I wasn't able to fully understood what he meant that time.

In a more traditional sense, leverage can be interpreted as having a greater impact or reach with the same, or sometimes less, amount of effort. The book you are reading now is a form of leverage that I have built, it took a while to write but the value and sales it continues to garner will continue to outwork me. I can sell this book anywhere around the world online and the website I built around it will continue to bring in leads while I sleep. The time it took to write the book is not directly correlated to the amount of value it can bring.

It could be a digital product you built, an online tutorial or even an ecommerce website. Digital products give you unlimited leverage as it continues to work outside the hours you put in it.

It could also mean having access to influential people or clients that no one else does. This substantially increases your value to a company because you have the potential to bring in more clients. For example, if you were in the business of selling houses and had connections with athletes, actors, or politicians who could afford million-dollar homes, you would have leverage.

There are many forms of leverage but in a nutshell leverage allows you to scale your impact and reach with an unfair advantage within your means. This concept was difficult for me to accept because I didn't feel like I had any unique advantages that could increase my impact. At least not yet. But then I realised that there are two types of leverage: Permissioned and Permissionless Leverage.

Types of Leverage

Permissioned leverage refers to the traditional forms of leverage. It typically involves relying on physical assets or third-party individuals for permission to do something. For instance, if you were a chef looking to open your own restaurant, you would need capital from a bank, as well as construction workers, engineers, architects, and employees to make it happen. You would also need assistance with legalities and marketing efforts. Each step in building a restaurant requires some form of permissioned leverage, or in other words, someone has to give you permission to do it usually in exchange for capital.

On the other hand, Permissionless Leverage is about creating your own opportunities without needing external validation or permission. Let's say our chef from before takes a different path and realises that many restaurants still use pen and paper for customer orders and struggle with excess food waste. He comes up with the idea of building an application to address these issues, knowing that other restaurants likely have similar problems. He either learns how to code or hires an engineer to bring his application to life. As more restaurants start using his app for inventory management and selling excess food online, he earns a 10% cut from each transaction. He built the application once and it continues to grow, allowing him to scale his impact without working for any specific restaurant. Permissionless leverage enables you to build something on your own terms, without seeking permission, and potentially achieve greater impact.

Here are other examples of permissionless leverage:

- Designing a mobile app
- Starting a podcast
- Creating an online course
- Launching a YouTube channel
- Developing a software tool
- Creating a graphic novel
- Starting a blog
- Developing an e-commerce website
- Launching a photography business
- Selling stock photos
- Designing and selling merchandise online

Permissionless leverage often involves building something once and reaping asymmetrical rewards. It grants you control over your life, which is what many nomad entrepreneurs strive for. We become entrepreneurs because we crave freedom – the freedom to control our own destinies. We're willing to work harder than in traditional 9-to-5 jobs for the chance to break free from working for someone else and spending decades chained to our desks.

Disconnect Time from Income

One of the advantages of Permissionless Leverage is that it doesn't require continuous physical labor in order to generate income. We often associate "work" with strenuous physical activity, but this isn't always the case. Consider a software engineer who creates an application that's downloaded worldwide for $5.99 per download. The engineer built it once, yet it continues to generate thousands of dollars every month as its reach expands globally. Build once, earn multiple times.

Take a moment and think about the last app you purchased without hesitation because you needed it – perhaps it was a weather app, a stock tracking tool, or a mortgage calculator. If millions of people had a similar thought and downloaded the app, the developer would earn millions of dollars and these endeavours aren't overly complex to create.

Similarly, imagine a YouTuber who records videos of his travels, showcasing the sights and sounds of Bali. You stumble upon his video while planning your own trip to Bali and watch it without giving much thought, with of course, the 30-second commercial at the beginning. That YouTuber just earned $1.00 while enjoying his vacation in Bali. Now imagine that millions of people visit Bali each year and watch the same video – that YouTuber could amass millions of dollars simply by documenting his vacation.

The great thing about permissionless leverage is that it continues working for you even when you're not actively working on it. The software engineer built the app once and it operates 24/7 with unlimited reach. People from all over the world can access it at any time, without constraints like physical presence or limited hours in a day. Similarly, content creators aren't limited to one platform – if YouTube doesn't support their content, there are numerous other platforms where they can share their work. The potential for success is limitless.

As a side note, this is not to remove the effort it took to actually get started and to the time it takes to build traction. Yes, once your asset starts earning while you sleep it becomes a lot easier but to get to that point it will take some time and dedication. For your videos to actually get viewers and a strong following, it will take some form of mastery of videography. There is no shortcut, there is no magic pill, it takes a craftsmanship mind shift to focus on building these digital products.

Number of Hotdogs Sold

On the other hand, permission leverage – like running a hotdog stand in Times Square – has inherent limitations. Regardless of how many people pass by on your hotdog stand, there's only so much you can sell in a day due to physical constraints. Suppose you can only sell and cook 100 hotdogs daily because of your cart's size and cooking time limitations. That means your maximum daily earnings are capped at $1,000 if you sold them at $1 each. This upper limit is tied to factors such as your physical presence and how well you market your stand – factors beyond your control. In this scenario, there will never be an instance of earning $100,000 in one day, even if a hundred thousand people showed up, unless you can suddenly scale yourself to be able to cook 10x hotdogs, you would have start hiring other vendors to cook for you which is a form of permissioned leverage.

Permissionless leverage isn't bound by such constraints. Once you create an application or video, it operates around-the-clock with unlimited potential reach. Whether people need a weather app or travel advice for Bali, your creation can cater to their needs. Even if you earn less than $1 per view or download, the sheer number of people in the world multiplies your scale, there is no limit on the upside. Unlike permissioned leverage, permissionless leverage isn't limited by time or external validation.

When embarking on the entrepreneurial journey, carefully consider whether you're pursuing permissioned or permissionless leverage. Think deeply about which path you want to take because the effort required, regardless of the chosen path, is significant. The effort it takes to work in a 100 million market is the same effort it takes to work in 1 million market.

Chapter Summary: Build Leverage

- Leverage is about multiplying impact or reach.
- There are two types of leverage: permissioned and permissionless.
- Permissioned leverage involves relying on physical assets or third-party individuals for permission to do something.
- Permissionless leverage is about creating your own opportunities without external validation or permission.
- Permissionless leverage allows you to build something on your own terms and potentially achieve greater impact.
- Permissionless leverage often involves building something once and reaping asymmetrical rewards.
- It disconnects time from income, allowing for passive income generation.
- Permission leverage has inherent limitations, such as physical constraints and limited earning potential.
- Permissionless leverage is not bound by these constraints and has unlimited potential reach.

Build Credibility

"Reputation is like fine china, once broken it can be mended, but the cracks will always remain." - Unknown

Show your Work

Building credibility is a critical skill that everyone should know how to do, especially if you want to be an entrepreneur and take control of your life and time. No matter how talented you are, if nobody sees your work, it will all be in vain. That's why marketing and sharing your work is crucial in order to get known for what you do.

One way to effectively build credibility is by showing your work. Instead of focusing solely on building your product and then seeking an audience, the concept of "showing your work" encourages you to build an audience while building. By constantly sharing your progress, being open about the challenges you face, and seeking feedback and support along the way, you can build a loyal following. The phrase *"Show your work" is* something I learned from the book by *Austin Kleon* of the same title, essentially argues that rather than first focusing on building your product and then start find an audience, he shows that the other way is to build an audience while building by showing your work.

Building in public is a popular approach to showing your work. Rather than keeping your work hidden until it's ready for public consumption, building in public involves being transparent about the process and progress. This allows you to engage with your target niche community and better understand their pain points.

Live the Life

When I was writing this book, I made sure to live the life of a nomad entrepreneur myself. I didn't want to write about a lifestyle I hadn't experienced or spoken to others who have lived it. Personal experience is invaluable when it comes to sharing insights and advice. However, my own experiences alone weren't enough to justify writing this book. That's why I also sought out other nomads and entrepreneurs, speaking with them and understanding their unique journeys and challenges. By connecting with like-minded individuals in communities dedicated to these lifestyles, I gained access to more data points and was able to draw more well-rounded conclusions.

We also had started our own YouTube channel to showcase how it is to live around the world, essentially showing to the world that the values that the book covers here actually works and our own way of showing our work.

Search "Aey and Mel" if you're interested to see where the values from the book has taken us, and leave a comment that you've found our channel from this book, we love connecting with like-minded people.

As a Software Engineer, I connect with other engineers from around the world. This allows me to better understand the decisions they make in their applications and learn from their experiences. In turn, I share my own resources and insights through articles about new technologies or lessons learned while building my own applications. This not only helps build credibility within the engineering community but also fosters a sense of community and collaboration.

Marketing strategies may vary depending on the industry you're in. For example, construction professionals might share video tutorials on YouTube to establish an online presence, while brain surgeons might start podcasts to broaden their reach. Regardless of your industry, it's crucial to prioritise building credibility in whatever way suits your field. Don't hide your work; instead, showcase it to the world. By doing so, you not only increase your potential for success but also enable yourself to scale and reach new heights.

Chapter Summary: Build Credibility

- Marketing is a critical skill for entrepreneurs to gain visibility and credibility.
- Building an audience while building your product is a powerful strategy.
- Building in public, being open about your progress, and seeking feedback are effective ways to build credibility.
- Engaging with your target niche community helps you understand their pain points.
- Personal experience and connecting with like-minded individuals provide valuable insights for writing a book or sharing knowledge.
- Connecting with professionals in your industry can help you gain credibility and gather information.
- Different industries require different marketing strategies, but the importance of building credibility remains consistent.
- Not sharing your work limits your ability to scale and hinders your unique potential.

Measure Progress

"Progress is impossible without change, and those who cannot change their minds cannot change anything." - George Bernard Shaw

What You Do

When you become an entrepreneur, the rewards can be asymmetrical and exponential. For example, you might go for almost four years with consistently close to zero income each year, and then suddenly, in year five, your business takes off. You gain a million customers who are willing to pay for the product or service you've been offering for the past four years. This is why many business owners quit – they run out of capital during the down times or simply lose hope. The years of receiving almost zero validation can be brutal and not everyone can manage it. It can damage your self-esteem when you continuously show up every day to do quality work but have nobody believe in you. This is especially true if most of your life you've been accustomed to having a monthly income, and it can come as an extreme shock.

This feeling then is exacerbated by friends and family who often throw words of discouragement your way when you start your own business. They assume that you are bound to fail and give advice like "just get a job." Over time, this erodes our internal perception of ourselves and we begin to question if we are wasting our lives. It becomes even harder to sustain as society looks down on us further. We must understand that this path is less traveled and those accustomed to linear progress and validation simply cannot comprehend exponential returns. People with traditional jobs who receive a steady stream of recurring paycheques are constrained by those upper limits and cannot fathom a world where asymmetries occur.

Regardless of the math and potential returns we can make as entrepreneurs, there is no denying that going against societal norms is no easy feat. It becomes difficult to engage in social situations when the conversation starts with "so what do you do?"and you receive condescending looks once you explain about your business venture that isn't gaining much traction. This is why most entrepreneurs say surround yourself with people that are also in the 'arena', those aiming to become entrepreneurs themselves. The path becomes more bearable once you are surrounded with other people doing what you do, rather than being surrounded by naysayer. The negativity will get you.

It's interesting how once you do become a successful entrepreneur, everyone flocks to you wanting to figure out how you achieved success. Be especially prepared when they do a complete 180 and start saying "I knew you always had it in you". The societal benefits become asymmetrical and exponential as well – nobody pays attention to you when you're starting out, but all the lights are on you in the end. You just need to weather the storm in the beginning, just know that it gets better at the end.

Focus on Internal Growth

Another skillset that can help combat these challenges is the ability to measure progress. The main idea is to shift the validation of your self-worth from external sources to something internal. For example, let's say you're an aspiring content creator. If you measure your progress solely by likes and subscribers, it can demoralise you if you create quality video content month after month without seeing external validation, e.g: getting subscribers and/or views. Instead, measure how well you're producing your videos – are you improving your speaking skills? Are you getting better at video editing? Are you able to create quality thumbnails now? Have you improved your copyrighting skills and learned how to best describe your videos? By shifting your focus, the number of subscribers and views becomes a measure of self-growth. When people ask 'what you do', you can confidently say that you're becoming a skilled video editor or a proficient public speaker because that's what it truly is. When you grow internally, it feeds your self-esteem and allows you to not rely the external for your sense of self-worth allowing you to keep doing what you are doing.

Which do you find more fulfilling and would be more likely to share:

A) "I got 1000 subscribers" or

B) "I'm a video editor and produce stories"

Interestingly enough, the more internally focused we become, the more others begin to take notice – when people see our confidence and self-esteem, they are more likely to believe in us or become curious about what we do, feeding that positive feedback loop.

As an author, I don't measure my success solely by the number of sales or views my work receives. I measure it by the state of flow I achieve when I write, by the growth of my vocabulary that comes as a byproduct of writing, by my ability to journal every day regardless of how I'm feeling, by my improved ability to organise my thoughts on paper, and by the skill of conveying a specific thought or message more eloquently to others through writing.

As a software engineer, I don't measure myself solely by the number of tickets I resolve or the number of users I reach on my website. I measure myself by the quality of code I produce – if I know that I didn't cut corners and produced high-quality code even under pressure. I measure myself by whether or not I can safely share my code publicly, knowing that it's something I'm proud to have worked on. And if I can sleep at night knowing that I did my best in ensuring there are no bugs in the code I built. I measure myself if I'm constantly learning new technologies that allows me to stay up-to-date and not be subject to bias from old lessons learned years ago.

There are numerous ways to measure your progress and shift validation from external sources to internal ones. This skillset is a core competency because without this shift, it becomes harder to sustain an entrepreneurial path, especially with societal pressures and expectations about what the norm should look like.

Action Point: Take a moment to reflect. In your craft, how do you measure your own progress? How do you know if you are growing even if no one else is validating your growth?

Chapter Summary: Measure Progress

- Becoming an entrepreneur comes with asymmetrical and exponential rewards, but also years of almost zero validation and income.
- Many people quit entrepreneurship due to lack of validation and support from friends and family.
- Society often looks down on entrepreneurs, making it difficult to go against societal norms.
- The ability to measure progress is crucial for sustaining an entrepreneurial path.
- Shifting validation from external sources to internal growth is important.
- Measuring progress internally feeds self-esteem and confidence, which in turn attracts external validation.

Infinite Learning

"Education is the passport to the future, for tomorrow belongs to those who prepare for it today." - Malcolm X

Education Begins After Graduation

When was the last time you truly learned something new with childlike wonder without earning more as your motivation? When was the last time you delved deep into a completely different circle of knowledge that you were unfamiliar with? Often, we view education as something formal, a means to obtain a degree or certification. We see it as a way to increase our value within our corporate jobs, pursuing a Master's Degree or industry certification solely to ask for a pay raise in our 9-5 jobs. Education becomes a path to higher salary, transforming our earning potential from $30,000 to possibly $100,000 based on the degree we pursue during our collegiate years. And yet, we continue seeking more education in hopes of further increasing our salary. Rarely do we hear people say they went to universities simply for the sake of learning. Why would they? The cost of obtaining a formal degree has steadily increased over the years, making it difficult to justify pursuing education purely for the sake of knowledge. Obtaining a degree becomes a transaction: I take on debt to obtain a formal degree and in return, I should receive an increase in pay. It has become a transactional move.

Unfortunately, this perspective is skewed. Education is not something you complete in your twenties and then abandon once you secure employment. Even if we set aside entrepreneurship, education must remain a constant tool in your arsenal due to the rapid rate at which the world is evolving. Without staying up-to-date, you risk becoming obsolete every few years. The introduction of Artificial Intelligence has only accelerated this need for continuous learning. AI aims to disrupt most—if not all—industries and aims to reinvent how people work. While this may not be new information, it serves as a reminder that new technologies emerge regularly and change how we operate. For instance, just five years ago someone who had no interest in understanding new technologies would now be bewildered by technical terms that have become mainstream: cryptocurrency, blockchain, web3, and whatever other new technologies arise. This cycle of constant growth is not unique; in the previous generation the people were bewildered by the terms: email, cell phones, and the internet. Further that, terms like automobile, horsepower, and engines were once new to earlier generations. We are just in a constant state of trying to keep up with the latest wave of innovation.

Sweet Summer Child

When I first started my Software Engineering career, I was naive and obnoxious. I believed that engineering was the most complex field, and that understanding it would make it easier to dissect other industries. I thought of design and UX as trivial, simply involving colours, font sizes, and button placement. It all seemed straightforward to me. That is, until I had the opportunity to work with a master designer.

She introduced me to psychology models that explained how the brain works and how it can be manipulated to make people addicted to their phones (Search: Hook Model). It became clear that designing an application with addictive qualities by triggering dopamine hits through notifications or messages was an ethical issue. It was like designing a news feed that resembled slot machines in casinos, constantly enticing users to pull down for new updates and experience that rush of dopamine. But it was something I didn't see nor understood, it all felt like just bells and whistles without understanding the fundamentals.

Similarly, I used to think Sales and Marketing were simple. "Just build it, and they will come," I thought or heard somewhere. But this belief was naive because I had tried building many applications during my journey, only for no one to show up. The cold hard truth is that if nobody knows about your product or application, there's no way for them to buy it. Mastering Sales and Marketing meant a better understanding of what makes people tick and why people choose one brand versus another. It was much deeper than just putting a price to a product or asking people to buy something from you. Attention is a scarce resource that every conglomerate competes for, with companies spending millions of dollars just to capture people's attention. So how can you expect your new application to get noticed when you're up against such competition? Naturally, you can't. That's where marketing comes into play.

I learned that Marketers use various techniques to grab the attention of your target users. We've already discussed ads on social media platforms designed to appear harmless while we're engaged in them. But there are other tools in the marketing toolbox as well.

One such technique is flash sales, which create a sense of urgency among potential buyers. For example, limited-time offers like "only available in the next 24 hours" or "get 20% off if you buy now." But wait, there's more! If you purchase within the next 10 minutes, we'll add an additional 10% off just for you! This type of advertisement triggers a Fear Of Missing Out (FOMO) impulse, pushing us into reaction mode and preventing us from deliberating further about the potential purchase.

This urgency created by marketing removes our doubts about whether we actually wanted to buy the product in the first place. We think, "It's 30% off, that's a steal!" What we don't know is that the product may have already been selling at a 30% discount because it's unwanted stock or because its inflated price makes the actual value only 70%. When we don't pause and consider the actual value of a product due to marketing-induced urgency, we easily fall for these strategies. Then we come home and realise we shouldn't have made that purchase. Now it joins all the other unnecessary items in our garages or rooms that we thought were bargains but didn't really need.

There were so many things I started to see at a deeper level, from different industries and disciplines when I made the decision to learn from them out of curiosity.

Empower Yourself

How do I gain knowledge about different concepts employed in various industries such as design, sales, and marketing? The answer lies in education. However, it's not the conventional education that you might be thinking of. It's about being genuinely curious and wanting to understand how things work.

I remember a time when I was deceived by a marketer who used clever marketing techniques to create a false sense of urgency. This experience sparked my curiosity. I wanted to know how they were able to convince me into making a purchase that I later realised it contained a degree of psychological manipulation. It led me on a deep dive into various subjects, driven by my desire to avoid being tricked again.

When you don't educate yourself:

- You become trapped in your own perspective.
- You limit your potential by not expanding your knowledge.

There are many ways to educate yourself:

- Watch informative videos.
- Use the internet as a valuable resource.
- Take advantage of tutorials and guides.
- Embrace reinvention and continuous learning.
- Surround yourself with like-minded individuals
- Stay curious and always seek new knowledge.
- Strive to provide value in everything you do.

Understanding how the world works is like having a superpower. It liberates us from falling victim to the techniques employed by those around us. We recognise the hooks they use and the dopamine release they target, all with the aim of achieving their end goals. Education empowers us to see the world through a new lens and enables us to play at a different level.

We often upgrade our phones and televisions, but we neglect to upgrade our thinking patterns. We forget that our brains are like operating systems that need constant updates and improvements. In today's digital age, we have traded true learning and education for smartphones and other smart gadgets. It's up to us to educate ourselves continuously or risk being made a fool.

Chapter Summary: Infinite Learning

- Education is often viewed as a means to obtain a degree or certification for higher salary
- Education must be ongoing due to the rapid rate of change in the world
- Education is about being genuinely curious and wanting to understand how things work
- Lack of education traps us in our own perspective and limits our potential for growth
- Ways to educate ourselves include watching informative videos, using the internet as a resource, taking tutorials and guides, embracing continuous learning, surrounding ourselves with like-minded individuals, staying curious, and striving to provide value in everything we do
- Education empowers us to see the world through a new lens and play at a different level

Be Formless

Laws of Power

When I was a kid, I saw a video of Jet Li talking about the secret of power. He said, "Empty your mind, be formless, shapeless - like water. Now you put water into a cup, it becomes the cup; you put water into a bottle, it becomes the bottle; you put it in a teapot, it becomes the teapot. Now water can flow or it can crash. Be water, my friend" At the time, I didn't understand what he meant. Did being like water mean making your limbs go limp to become more powerful? Was it a superpower that allowed punches to go through you? My young mind couldn't grasp the concept, but I held onto the idea of being like water in fights because Jet Li spoke about it and it sounded cool. It stayed at the back of my mind, even though I didn't fully understand it.

As a younger adult, I read the book *48 Laws of Power* by *Robert Greene*. The last law in the book was "Be formless and unpredictable." The first and last laws in any list usually hold much weight since they are often considered the best and most impactful. I wondered why Robert Greene chose to end his book with this law. Once again, there was a small correlation to what Jet Li had said about being like water, but I still couldn't fully grasp why this was such a powerful law. It remained in the back of my mind without much clarity.

It wasn't until I entered the real world that everything started to make sense. I realised that environments, people, time - everything had its own form or shape.

Real-World Application

When you work for different companies, you realise that it's not just a place where you go to work; there are shapes you need to fit into in order to thrive. These shapes come in the form of values, mission statements, and vision statements that companies publicly display. But there are also internal shapes within companies - unspoken rules that everyone knows or should know. Rules like "We don't just work 9-5 here" or "We don't talk back to senior executives." These rules are never written anywhere, not in your contract or the company values, but they are implicit expectations that you are expected to know and obey.

When you interact with people from certain demographics or upbringings, there is pressure to fit in. For example, in certain parts of the world, the common expectation for the next generation is to achieve a certain profession like being a doctor or lawyer. Anything else may be considered a failure or not the optimal outcome for their definition of success. There are also societal pressures that come with it - expectations like not talking back to adults regardless of their age, or not being able to get promoted higher than someone older than you regardless of your competencies. These are the shapes of societal norms, and there's no handbook or internet guide to learn them; you're just expected to know.

Formlessness, or being "like water," makes sense in a bigger context. It was never just about fighting; it was about understanding how the world works. If you can be formless, you can easily adapt to any environment you're thrown into. You don't force yourself into different environments like trying to fit a square peg into a round hole; instead, you thrive in any and all environments. As an entrepreneur, you're not constrained by current trends or your preexisting view of the world. You can pivot and make necessary changes to how you view the world and what its current shape is. In most cases, it becomes absolutely necessary to be able to quickly pivot from one shape to another because of the constantly changing demands of the world.

Changing Shape

When I started my career as a software engineer, I believed it was all about technology and coding. My shape was that of a software engineer, and I looked at the world through that lens. Everything I saw was tech-related, and I paid close attention to movements in the tech industry. Only when I had the courage to let go of those constraints did I truly understand how the world worked.

I learned about leverage, sales, marketing, entrepreneurship, and even writing a book. If I had stuck to my technical lens, none of these other aspects would have made sense in the world of pure coding, and I would have dismissed them as a waste of my time. If I had confined myself to being just a software engineer, I would only thrive in places, with people, and at events that accommodated that specific shape. Anything else would have been a struggle for me. It was tough to accept that in today's age, especially now where being an engineer could easily be replaced with Artificial Intelligence and I thought that it shouldn't solely define my identity.

Only when we let go of preconceived notions and prior lessons can we truly adapt. This is one of the core competencies of being a nomad entrepreneur - the ability to adapt to different places and adjust your business ventures to the current shape of the world while still thriving *and traveling*. We must be unafraid to let go of our self-imposed molds and be able to adjust and reinvent ourselves.

When we cling hard to a mold we've set for ourselves, it becomes difficult to make necessary adjustments and blinds us to the realities of the world. If we label ourselves as homeowners or doctors or restaurant owners or even specific places, like New Yorkers, it becomes challenging to consider alternative options or paths because we're fixated on our predetermined shapes. Only when we can let go and be completely formless can we thrive in this continuously changing world.

As Jet Li once said: "Be like water, my friend."

Action Point: Take a moment to reflect. What do you identify yourself as when presenting yourself to the world? The answer often comes in the form of your response when someone asks you "What do you do?" Is this shape you see yourself in a rigid constraint? What happens if the world decides this shape or form is no longer relevant? What comes next?

Chapter Summary: Be Formless

- "Be like water" - the concept of formlessness and adaptability
- Environments, people, and time have shapes or forms
- Social Pressure to fit in certain societal expectations and norms
- Being formless allows for adaptation to any environment
- Constraints of identity can limit growth and understanding of the world
- Core competency of a nomad entrepreneur is adaptability and reinvention
- Letting go of preconceived notions and labels allows for necessary adjustments
- Thriving in a continuously changing world requires being formless

PART 4: TRAVEL

Insurances Fallacies

"The greatest enemy of knowledge is not ignorance, it is the illusion of knowledge." - Stephen Hawking

The Squeeze

In my opinion, health insurance is similar to wearing a seat belt on a plane ride. While it may not actually save your life in the event of a crash, it often provides a false sense of security. While seatbelts help in certain situations, such as preventing you from being tossed around during flight turbulence, the chances of it saving your life in a plane crash is minuscule to non-existent. The same principle applies to health insurances. I have some skepticism towards insurances due to past negative experiences. I would consistently pay for insurance year after year, only to encounter loopholes or complications when I actually needed coverage. It always seemed that the more expensive options covered 95 out of 100 possible diseases, and I would end up getting sick with one of the five that were explicitly not covered.

Just like casinos, the [insurance] house always wins. Why wouldn't they? Companies have actuaries who calculate statistics based on your demographic and potential diseases you could develop and impose multiple prerequisites before paying out for illnesses that are more likely to occur. This is simply how the business operates, otherwise they would go bankrupt if they had to pay for everyone's hospitalisation. They offer coverage for a long list of illnesses that are less likely to occur in reality. As a result, when you do get sick with a common illness, there is a high chance that they won't cover your medical bills, regardless of how long you've been with them.

Despite my reservations about insurances, I still purchase them because even though most sicknesses covered are unlikely to happen, there's still a small chance that an event with significant consequences could occur. For example, if Disease A is covered but only has a 5% chance of occurring, but the hospital bills could amount to $1 million dollars if it does happen, the small chances convinces me to pay for insurance.

Don't Sweat the Small Stuff

Nassim Nicholas Taleb suggests in his book *Antifragile: Things That Gain from Disorder* that it's wise to take insurances only on potentially life-devastating events and accept risks that result in negligible material losses. People often insure things that don't significantly impact their bottom line due to clever marketing by retailers. For example, warranties for phones are often promoted with fear tactics, making you think your phone will break soon after purchasing it or a year after purchase. The reality is that the chances of breaking your phone within a year plus the ability to return it to the store are minimal. The chances of you forgetting that you have your phone insured, misplacing the insurance details, or even purchasing a new phone are all more likely to occur than returning it within a year, and these are what these insurers are betting on.

In our fast-paced lives, it's easy to overlook the fact that we have insurance coverage for our phones. With so many things vying for our attention, it's not surprising that we may forget about this important protection. Additionally, keeping track of the specific details regarding our insurance can be a challenge. It's not uncommon to misplace or forget where we stored these documents.

In reality, the money spent on unnecessary warranties could have been used for something more valuable. However, the sheer number of "small" insurances people constantly pay for starts to compound, with insurances available for everything ranging from minor inconveniences to major hassles, it all then becomes a big chunk of money that goes out our accounts without adding true value into our lives.

Conjunction Fallacies

Some insurances are designed to overlap. For example, if you have health insurance that covers sicknesses, why would you need separate travel insurance? Does that mean you're only covered on your health when not traveling? What about when you're in transit or on a plane? Specialised insurances are designed to make you feel especially covered in certain situations when general insurances do the job.

Take this mental exercise: If you we're going to be skiing in the alps, which is a better insurance: 'Ski & Snowboarding Insurance' or 'Travel Insurance'? The answer should have been travel insurance, unless they explicitly say they don't cover snow accidents. It becomes more inclusive of all possibilities, from before getting to the Alps to getting food poisoning at the cafeteria there or falling from the ski lift. The former insurance actually imposes more risk to you because it only covers ski and snowboarding related accidents. When taking insurance the aim is to get covered with the most amount of risks involved that can essentially wipe you out financially, whether known or unknown. It's also worth noting that airlines also sell insurance if you get sick during a flight. Wouldn't that have been covered in a regular travel insurance already?

If you take out every possible insurance available, it can quickly add up. It's important to be aware of events that are unlikely but could have significant consequences if they do occur compared to events that are more likely but won't impact your life as much as you fear.

When it comes to being a nomad and traveling, the worst-case scenario is getting sick in a country where you can't afford the medical bills. Even though the chances may be less than 1%, if it were to happen, it could leave you broke and in debt for the rest of your life. In this case, getting coverage is recommended.

If you're considering insurance as part of your journey, here are some guideposts that can point you in the right direction:

Which is Better: Credit Card Insurance or Health Insurance?

Again, another a simple thought experiment. In the real world, which option would you likely choose? Here are the coverage options for credit cards and health/travel insurances:

Typical Health Insurance List of Coverage:

- Blood
- Bone, joint and muscle
- Brain and nervous system
- Breast surgery (medically necessary)
- Kidney and bladder
- Chemotherapy, radiotherapy and immunotherapy for cancer
- Dental surgery
- Diabetes management (excluding insulin pumps)

- Tonsils, adenoids and grommets
- Digestive system
- Ear, nose and throat
- Eye (not cataracts)
- Gastrointestinal endoscopy
- Gynaecology
- Heart and vascular system
- Hernia and appendix
- Skin
- Implantation of hearing devices
- Lung and chest Joint reconstructions
- Male reproductive system
- Miscarriage and termination of pregnancy
- Pain management
- Plastic and reconstructive surgery (medically necessary)
- Podiatric surgery* (provided by an accredited podiatric surgeon)
- Emergency Ambulance
- Hospital psychiatric services
- Rehabilitation
- Palliative care
- Joint replacement
- Pregnancy and birth
- Assisted reproductive services
- Dialysis for chronic kidney failure
- Cataracts Weight loss surgery Insulin pump
- Back, neck, and spine

Credit Card Coverage:

- All Medical Expenses Covered

If you're a cautious person like me, you take extra time to consider obvious choices. Leading questions often have an underlying motive and when faced with an obvious answer, I purposely choose the non-obvious one just to challenge the leading question. Therefore, I can't assume what the obvious answer is for you as the reader. However, I do know that most people would choose the first option.

When selecting health insurance, people often fall victim to cognitive biases such as the "Conjunction Fallacy" or "Conjunction Effect," popularised by *Nassim Nicholas Taleb* in his book *Fooled by Randomness: The Hidden Role of Chance in Life and in the Markets*.

The extensive list of coverage in the first option often makes us believe it's the better choice. It appears comprehensive, and as a potential buyer, I assume they have covered everything necessary. If there's something missing from the list, it's likely because those diseases are less likely to happen or warrant you to remember what. Most insurance websites go the extra mile to list as many variations of diseases as possible, often longer than the list I provided here. However, upon further inspection, it becomes clear that the second option is actually superior. The simplicity of "All medical expenses covered" eliminates the need for a long list of specific diseases. In fact, the long list may have purposely omitted common diseases with higher probabilities to reduce the chances of payouts by insurance companies.

Conjunction Effect occurs when people believe that the combination of two specific events or conditions is more likely than either event or condition occurring individually. In our previous example, when we see a long list of diseases, our brain subconsciously adds up the occurrence probabilities of each disease. For example, what is the chance of needing treatment for Bone, Joint and Muscle (10%) + Ear, Nose and Throat (5%) + Emergency Ambulance (20%) + Cataracts (10%) + and so on? Without further thought, we implicitly assume that since the probability exceeds 100%, we are more likely to need treatment for multiple diseases listed.

Credit cards rarely promote their travel insurance coverage because it's not their main selling point. However, credit cards targeted towards travellers often offer a bundle of benefits worth considering.

As a digital nomad, my credit card provided me with threefold benefits: frequent flyer points for discounted flights and lounge access, quick cash overseas if needed, and a comprehensive travel insurance that covers all medical expenses. Many credit cards with higher interest rates come with insurance packages, especially those focused on travel. Check your existing credit cards to see if they offer these benefits or if there's an option to upgrade your package. Consider the math: if paying a bit more on your credit card can provide the same or even more comprehensive coverage than purchasing additional health insurance, it's worth exploring that route. Each individual has access to different providers that may offer what you're looking for. Instead of getting a credit card, buying health insurance, and then trying to earn points on specific airlines, why not combine all three with one payment?

Be conscious of what you're paying for and the services already provided by your credit card, as not all credit cards are created equal.

Businesses often rely on consumers' lack of knowledge to sell unnecessary insurances. Take control of your finances and read the fine print!

Nomad Insurances

If you're not convinced about getting a credit card or if you know yourself as someone who easily falls into debt when they do have one, there are other options available.

As the world becomes more open to digital nomads and countries embrace the idea of global citizenship, insurances are adapting to cater specifically to this market. There are several insurances targeted towards nomads that provide coverage across various locations worldwide. Simply search for "Nomad Insurance" or "Nomad Health Insurance" and research which option best suits your situation.

Some people suggest that a good rule of thumb is to choose an insurance plan with the highest excess or deductible (or lowest monthly rate). This means that if you were hospitalised, out of all the packages offered by the insurance, the one with the lowest monthly rate would require you to pay the largest amount out of pocket before the insurance covers the rest. The rationale behind this is that when considering odds, you would have paid much more in monthly fees than the excess required in case of hospitalisation. The likelihood of being hospitalised is lower but monthly fees are constant and guaranteed. However, everyone has their own threshold and considerations when choosing insurance. Deep-diving into the topic of probability and statistics relative to your circumstances is beyond the scope of this book. However, I will provide appendices for further readings if you're interested.

Chapter Summary: Insurance Fallacies

- Health insurances provide a false sense of security and often have loopholes that prevent coverage when needed.
- Insurance companies calculate statistics and impose prerequisites to avoid paying out for common illnesses.
- Despite skepticism, purchasing insurance is still worthwhile for potential high-cost medical bills.
- Many people are misled by the conjunction fallacy when selecting health insurance, assuming more coverage is better.
- Credit cards often offer comprehensive travel insurance as a benefit, which can be a better option than separate health insurance.
- Nomad insurances specifically target digital nomads and provide coverage in various locations globally.
- It may be beneficial to choose an insurance plan with a higher deductible or excess to save on monthly fees if hospitalisation is unlikely.

Two Factor Affliction

"In preparing for battle I have always found that plans are useless, but planning is indispensable." - Dwight D. Eisenhower

The Two-Factor Affliction is a common challenge faced by global citizens, and it is caused by a simple technical innovation called 2FA or Two-Factor Authentication. As you travel around the world, you will encounter varying methods of connecting to the internet, often leading to frequent changes of sim cards. While using local sim cards may be the cheaper option for mobile connectivity, it poses a problem for online banking.

Your online bank accounts are typically linked to your local phone number, which becomes an issue when you switch sim cards. This makes it difficult to log into your accounts because you are unable to receive the necessary 6-digit code required by banks for login. Disabling 2FA is not recommended as it would make your accounts vulnerable to hacks and theft.

One particularly challenging situation arises when you are in a country with no reception and need to access your bank accounts. In such cases, obtaining the required code becomes impossible, leaving you stranded.

Fortunately, there are global eSim providers available nowadays. It is advisable to do thorough research and choose the provider that best suits your location needs. Some providers only cover specific locations, so make sure to pick one that caters to your destination. Before embarking on your travels, take the proactive step of updating your bank account settings with a global sim number instead of relying on your local one. Alternatively, if possible, consider switching to email-based two-factor authentication.

This simple move can save you from experiencing the frustration of spending hours on hold trying to reach your bank from across the world while being unable to access your funds.

Chapter Summary: Two Factor Affliction

• The Two-Factor Affliction is caused by Two-Factor Authentication (2FA)

• Using local sim cards while traveling can cause difficulties with online banking

• Local sim cards make it difficult to receive the necessary 6-digit code for login

• Disabling 2FA is not recommended for security reasons

• In countries with no reception, accessing bank accounts becomes impossible

• Global eSim providers are available to solve this issue

• Choose a provider that suits your location needs before traveling

• Update bank account settings with a global sim number or consider email-based 2FA

• This proactive step can save time and frustration when accessing funds while traveling.

Stay Longer

"The best way to live a fulfilling life is to slow down, enjoy the journey, and appreciate the little moments along the way." - Oprah Winfrey

Economies of Scale

When it comes to travel, it is often more beneficial to stay in one house, BnB, or hotel for an extended period rather than constantly moving from one location to another within the same country.

Logistically, check-in times are typically around 2pm or 3pm, and in some cases can be as late as 4pm or 5pm. On the other hand, check-out times are usually around 10am or 11am. This means that during the gap between check-out and check-in, which can be a couple of hours, you may find yourself with all your luggage and nowhere to go. Depending on your situation and location, this can be quite inconvenient.

Not only does constantly moving from place to place require additional time and effort for packing and unpacking, but it also involves booking taxis or transportation between each location. These logistical factors can quickly add up, especially if the new location is not far off or significantly different from the previous one.

Additionally, staying in one place for an extended period allows you to access discounted prices. This concept is known as "Economies of Scale" and is a fundamental principle of economics. Just like how retail businesses buy products at discounted prices from suppliers and sell them at a profit, staying longer in one place often leads to lower accommodation costs. This principle applies to various industries - even taxes offer lower rates for stocks held for over a year compared to those bought and sold within a short timeframe. Banks even offer higher interest rates for larger account balances compared to maintaining smaller amounts. To be able to sustain this lifestyle you must be aware and take advantage of this principle, it sounds counterintuitive at first but staying longer actually is cheaper in the long run.

If you stay in one place for months on end, you may receive discounts or access certain exclusive benefits. For example, consistently booking flights with the same airline provider can grant privileges such as access to airport lounges and discounted flights. Similarly, booking through platforms like Airbnb up to a month can sometimes result in 20-50% discounts. Staying longer in one place allows you to start planning your meals and buying in bulk in groceries rather than eating out all the time. As an entrepreneur, it only makes sense to take advantage of opportunities to access the same value at a lower price. Why pay more when there is no need to?

Global Sense of Belonging

Staying in one place for an extended period not only offers economic advantages but also helps you better acclimate and develop a sense of home. As you become a regular at local cafes, restaurants, and shops, the people there begin to recognise and familiarise themselves with you. This recognition fosters a feeling of belongingness.

During our stay in Vietnam, we frequented a particular local restaurant for brunch due to its quality food. Over time, the owner started recognising us because of our frequent visits. It became an enjoyable experience every time we went as she welcomed us like old friends. She would make a grand gesture upon our arrival, announcing our presence to her cooks and staff. Other guests would often wonder who we were and why we received such a warm welcome compared to other regular tourists, which made us feel even more welcomed.

In addition to this restaurant, similar experiences occurred in other places we frequented during our travels. As we visited more locations, we found that business owners and locals recognised us, making us feel like true global citizens. Everywhere we went, it felt like we belonged somewhere simply because we had stayed in one place for a bit longer each time.

Chapter Summary: Stay Longer

- Staying in one place for longer periods of time in travel can be more convenient logistically, as check-in and check-out times can create temporary homelessness with luggage.

- Moving from one place to another requires time, effort, and logistical arrangements such as booking taxis and packing/unpacking.

- Staying in one place longer can lead to discounts and benefits, similar to the concept of "Economies of Scale" in economics.

- Accommodations may offer discounts or exclusive benefits for longer stays, airlines may provide privileges like airport lounge access and discounted flights for loyal customers, and platforms like Airbnb may offer discounts for repeat or longer bookings.

- Staying in one place longer helps create a sense of belonging as local businesses recognise and welcome you.

- Familiarity with cafes, restaurants, shops, etc. can make you feel like a local or global citizen rather than a tourist.

- Being recognised by locals and receiving warm welcomes makes you feel like you belong wherever you go.

Off Peak

"Take control of your own destiny, or someone else will." - Jack Welch

Forced Leave

One of the things that I despised about working for someone else was being forced to take a Christmas break. Now, don't get me wrong, I love spending Christmas with my family. But what really bothered me was the fact that I had no choice in the matter. The company would shut down for the holidays, and I was expected to do the same while using *my* annual leaves. It felt like my vacation time was being controlled by someone else, and it didn't sit well with me.

Imagine this: you have a limited number of vacation days in a year, let's say 20. And half of those days are already predetermined by your employer because you have to take them during their designated holiday break. So essentially, you only have 10 days of vacation that you can actually use when it suits you best.

But here's the kicker - everyone else is also on their forced Christmas break. And when demand is high, prices skyrocket. So if you want to travel during this time and visit your family or go on a holiday, everything becomes ridiculously expensive. Flights, accommodations, even food - all at exorbitant prices just because it happens to be a certain month and everyone else is on vacation. It's a lose-lose situation for the worker, you limited time to go on vacation while the prices are sky high, and it's forced on you.

When we were on our trip to Santorini Greece. We went during the off-peak season, which was a bit risky in terms of weather. But guess what? The lower prices allowed us to stay much longer than we could have during peak season. Yes, we had some bad weather days, but we also got to experience the best views Greece had to offer with minimal people around crowding the place at a fraction of the cost. It was a win-win situation for us.

On the other hand, when someone forces you to take your vacation during peak seasons, it becomes a lose-lose game. You're gambling with big money for the perfect weather while dealing with overcrowded spaces and incredibly expensive food prices.

People who work for themselves have full control, go to the best places in the world at a lowered price whenever they want. They are not dictated by an arbitrary season enforced by someone to be vacation time for the masses. Entrepreneurs find business on peak holiday season and go on vacation whenever and wherever they want.

So why settle for forced Christmas breaks when you can have the freedom to enjoy your holidays on your own terms? As an entrepreneur, the choice is yours.

Chapter Summary: Off Peak

- Prices skyrocket during peak travel times when forced breaks occur
- Self-employed individuals have the freedom to travel to the best places in the world at lower prices whenever they want
- Entrepreneurs can find business opportunities during peak holiday seasons and take vacations on their own terms.

Golden Visas

Willy Wonka

When I was younger, I had no knowledge of golden visas and what they entailed. Like many others who are unaware of their existence, I was surprised to discover that there are actually golden visas available in various countries. These visas go by different names such as Elite Visa, Platinum Visa, or Golden Visas, but their purpose remains the same: These visas allow you to stay in a country almost indefinitely with access to best things they have to offer.

It sounds like a lottery or a golden ticket to *Willy Wonka's Chocolate Factory,* like something out of a fairy tale. Golden visas are visas from certain countries that grant instant citizenship or the right to stay in the country, given certain prerequisites. These prerequisites usually involve a significant amount of money changing hands between countries. For example, in some cases, it may require buying a house in the country with a minimum purchase amount that is usually much higher than the average person can afford from that country. In Spain or Bali, for instance, it could require buying $5 million worth of property depending on what the current legislation is. In other cases, it may simply involve paying the country a large sum of money directly. Each country has its own requirements for obtaining a Golden Visa, but regardless of which country you choose, the perks remain the same: tax privileges and the right to live in that country regardless of your birthplace. There is no skills assessment or language proficiency test; money usually does all the talking. When money talks, the world listens.

I was born in a relatively poorer third world country, so to even be considered for immigration to other countries, I had to jump through multiple hoops. This included undergoing skills assessments to determine if my skillsets and abilities were needed and up to par with their standards, as well as demonstrating proficiency in speaking English at the desired level. This process could be demoralising; it felt like applying for a job and having people scrutinise your worthiness to live life at a certain level. Little did I know that there was an alternative—a golden backstage pass.

Value and Money

Money truly is a neutral indicator of value. If you increase your value by acquiring high-demand skills or expertise, money naturally flows towards you. This aligns with one of the fundamental principles of economics: supply and demand. The more in demand you are and the fewer people who possess your unique skills or abilities, the more money you can command. And as your value increases, countries start opening their doors to you. Instead of going through the arduous process of convincing immigration agencies to allow you into their country, countries themselves begin enticing you to choose them as your new home by offering various perks and privileges, such as tax-free residence.

I have come across countries where golden visas include benefits like free hospitalisations, stays in luxurious hotels, and even access to personal nannies for the elderly. Some countries offer fixed tax rates or no taxes at all. I intentionally refrain from mentioning specific countries and their offerings here, as regulations may change in the future and make this information obsolete. However, the principle of supply and demand will always be at play: Golden Visas are offered to those who increase their value, and countries open their doors to high-value individuals. The specific perks may vary, but the underlying concept remains constant.

A Global Perspective

The rise of golden visas reflects the changing dynamics of our global society. In an increasingly interconnected world, borders are becoming more fluid, and traditional notions of citizenship are being challenged. People are no longer bound by geographic limitations; they can now transcend borders and forge new identities in different countries.

This shift towards global citizenship has its benefits and challenges. On one hand, it promotes cultural exchange, diversity, and innovation. It allows individuals from different backgrounds to come together, bringing their unique perspectives and experiences to create something truly extraordinary.

On the other hand, it raises questions about identity and belonging. As more people acquire multiple citizenships or choose to live in different countries at different times in their lives, the notion of national identity becomes blurred. What does it mean to be a citizen? Where do our loyalties lie? These are complex questions that require careful consideration as we navigate this new era of global mobility.

The Power of Choice

The concept of golden visas has opened up a world of possibilities for individuals like myself. It has provided an alternative pathway to freedom and opportunity, regardless of one's birthplace or background. No longer are we confined to the limitations imposed by our circumstances; we now have the power to choose where we want to live, work, and thrive.

For me, the idea of a golden visa represents more than just a ticket to a new country; it symbolises the ability to create a better life for oneself and one's family. It is an opportunity to escape the constraints of poverty and embrace a future filled with promise and prosperity.

As in anything in life, things worth of value requires hard work. In order to be attain the privilege of accessing Golden visas requires you to increase the value you bring to society and in turn you gain the ability to live life at your own terms.

Whether we view Golden Visas as a golden ticket to Willy Wonka's Chocolate Factory or as a means to create a better life for ourselves, they represent a shift towards a more inclusive and interconnected world. As we navigate this new landscape, let us remember the power of choice, the value of money, and the importance of using our newfound freedom responsibly.

In the end, it is not just about obtaining a Golden Visa; it is about embracing the possibilities that come with it and making a positive impact on the world around us.

Chapter Summary: Golden Visas

- Golden visas are visas that grant instant citizenship or the right to stay in a country with certain prerequisites, usually involving a significant amount of money.
- Each country has its own requirements for obtaining a Golden Visa, but the perks remain the same: tax privileges and the right to live in that country regardless of birthplace.
- Money is a neutral indicator of value and increasing your value by acquiring high-demand skills or expertise can attract money and open doors to different countries.
- The rise of golden visas reflects the changing dynamics of our global society, where borders are becoming more fluid and traditional notions of citizenship are being challenged.
- Golden visas provide an alternative pathway to freedom and opportunity, allowing individuals to choose where they want to live, work, and thrive.
- Obtaining a golden visa requires increasing the value you bring to society and living life on your own terms.
- Golden visas represent a shift towards a more inclusive and interconnected world, where choices, money, and freedom are important considerations.
- It is not just about obtaining a golden visa; it is about embracing the possibilities that come with it and making a positive impact on the world.

PART 5: WHAT'S NEXT

Sneak Peek

I purposely structured this book from the perspective of a beginner because that's where I was when I wrote it. Despite my travels and experiences, I was still at the starting line of my journey as an entrepreneur. This book is a collection of things I wish I had known before becoming a global entrepreneur. When I first started, I had to piece together information from the internet, and often encountered skewed perspectives or hidden motives from those trying to influence me towards this lifestyle.

I wanted to begin the book by highlighting all the negatives and reasons why being a nomad may not be ideal. By presenting the nitty-gritty upfront, without romanticising the lifestyle, readers can make an informed decision about whether it's something they truly want to pursue. They will understand the trade-offs they need to make.

As my journey of a full-time nomad entrepreneur continues, I will document the lessons and mindset shifts I encounter along the way. These experiences will serve as key topics for my next book. If this book has provided any value to you as a reader, please show your support by leaving a review online or saying Hi to me on Twitter/X — it would mean the world to me.

Lastly, I'd like to give you a sneak peek of what life on this journey is like for the next upcoming book. Hope you enjoyed reading this as much as I enjoyed writing it in during our travels.

There is no "AHA" Moment

It's a Process

As you gain more experience as an entrepreneur and a nomad, you come to realise that there is no "AHA" moment. There was never a magical event that would instantly change your thinking or completely transform your reality. Whether you're traveling to find purpose and meaning or striving to become more fit and healthy, it's a slow and arduous process that requires consistent effort day in and day out.

Becoming more fit and healthy, for example, is not about going to the gym for 16 hours one day and waking up ripped the next. It's about consciously monitoring what you eat each day, pushing yourself to go to the gym even when you don't feel like it, and developing the mental strength to lift heavier weights with each session. It's the culmination of all these small activities and mindset shifts that ultimately lead to becoming the fit person you aspire to be. It's not just one thing or another; there must be synergy in everything you do.

The same principle applies to being a global entrepreneur. It's not about finding one product and selling it on a massive scale, chasing after every hot trend, or creating one viral piece of content. It's about gradually shifting your mindset and creating value that can potentially impact people's lives on a daily basis. It requires discipline and consistency, even when you're not seeing any immediate income for months on end or facing judgment from society or skepticism from friends and family. It involves cultivating a strong mental state and figuring out what works best for you in the chaos of this lifestyle.

There will never be a single event that transforms you from a 9-5 worker into a global entrepreneur; it's about making small incremental changes over time. The goal of this book is to contribute to your journey by providing valuable insights and putting you on solid footing when you actually start your entrepreneurial ventures. This book is not meant to make you say "AHA, I've read this book, now I'm ready to drop everything and go." That kind of instant transformation will never happen, and no single book can achieve that.

Exit Strategy

As in anything in life, it is important to have a clear vision of the end goal when starting something new. Going in blind without a sense of purpose can lead to confusion and loss of direction. Imagine attending school without a vision of eventually graduating or not understanding why you wanted to go to school in the first place. Similarly, joining a gym without knowing your fitness goals can result in aimless workouts and wasted time.

This lack of clarity can be seen in students who constantly change their majors or people who spend hours at the gym scrolling through their phones instead of working out. On the other hand, those who drop out of school early to pursue entrepreneurship or train themselves at home have a clear understanding of their goals and how these institutions will help them achieve success.

The same principle applies to being a nomad and an entrepreneur. Ask yourself what your ultimate goal is. Do you want to escape the corporate 9-5 job and avoid unnecessary meetings? Are you pursuing entrepreneurship as a means to support your family? Is it your desire to see the world or do you feel that staying in one country limits your experiences? Or all of the above?

Understanding your true motivations is crucial because there may be easier or more effective ways to achieve them. I have witnessed people becoming nomads without fully understanding why they were doing it, simply because they saw it online or thought it would be like a long vacation. However, being a nomad requires commitment and purpose; it is not just an extended holiday.

Take some time for introspection and reflection to determine what your exit strategy truly is. Are you hoping to continue traveling for the next 10-20 years, or is this journey just a stepping stone towards something bigger? Only you can answer this question, but it is important to gain clarity on your long-term goals.

And that, my fellow travellers, is my cue to Exit. Thank you for reading this book.

Appendix - Resources & Attribution

1. Nassim Nicholas Taleb. "The Black Swan: The Impact of the Highly Improbable." Publication Date: 2007, ISBN: 978-1400063512

2. Joshua Fields Millburn and Ryan Nicodemus. The Minimalists

3. Ramit Sethi. "I Will Teach You to Be Rich." Publication Date: 2009, ISBN: 978-0761147480

4. Napoleon Hill. "Think And Grow Rich." Publication Date: 1937, ISBN: 978-1585424337

5. Cal Newport. "Deep Work." Publication Date: 2016, ISBN: 978-1455586691

6. James Clear. "Atomic Habits" Publication Date: 2018, ISBN: 978-0735211292

7. Eric Jorgensen. "The Almanack of Naval Ravikant." Publication Date: 2020, ISBN: 978-1544514215

8. MJ DeMarco. "Millionaire Fastlane." Publication Date: 2011, ISBN: 978-0984358106

9. Daniel Kahnemann. "Thinking Fast & Slow" Publication Date: 2011, ISBN: 978-0374533557

10. Austin Kleon. "Show Your Work" Publication Date: 2014, ISBN: 978-0761178972

11. Nassim Nicholas Taleb "Antifragile: Things That Gain from Disorder." Publication Date 2014, ISBN: 978-0812979688

12. Nassim Nicholas Taleb. "Fooled by Randomness: The Hidden Role of Chance in Life and in the Markets." Publication Date: 2005, ISBN: 978-0812975215

13. Tim Ferris' 'Fear Setting' Exercise: https://tim.blog/2017/05/15/fear-setting/

14. https://www.psychologytoday.com/intl/blog/escaping-our-mental-traps/202206/overcoming-the-fear-public-speaking

15. http://www.theinvisiblegorilla.com/gorilla_experiment.html

About the Author

Melchor is an accomplished author, software engineer, and entrepreneur with a passion for sharing his knowledge and experiences with others. With a solid background in the technical world, Melchor has spent over 12 years working as a Software Engineer for various companies and industries. Through his work, he has not only gained expertise in his field but also developed a deep understanding of the needs and challenges faced by engineers.

Throughout his career, Melchor has been actively engaged in the engineering community as a writer, reaching millions of engineers through forums and online platforms. His insightful contributions have earned him recognition and respect among peers, establishing him as a trusted source of information in the technical world.

In addition to his professional achievements, Melchor embraces a dynamic lifestyle alongside his partner April. Together, they travel full time around the world while creating different business ventures. Having immigrated from the Philippines to Singapore, then finally settling in Australia while also working in the UK along their journey, Melchor and April have developed a global perspective that enriches their work and creative endeavours.

Driven by their desire for exploration and discovery, Melchor and April have made a commitment to document their extraordinary journey on YouTube. As streamers and full-time content creators, they captivate audiences with their diverse experiences and provide valuable insights into nomadic living, business development, and personal growth.

Melchor's unique blend of technical expertise, entrepreneurial spirit, and global perspective make him an invaluable resource for those seeking inspiration to pursue unconventional paths. As an author dedicated to empowering others with practical knowledge and real-life experiences, he continues to make significant contributions to both the engineering community and the world at large through his writing.